D0832681

lonely planet
Kids

HOW TO BE AN
INTERNATIONAL
SPY

Acknowledgements

Publishing Director   Piers Pickard
Commissioning Editor   Jen Feroze
Author   Andy Briggs
Illustrator   Ben Tobitt
Designer   Briony Hartley
In-house Senior
  Designer   Andy Mansfield
Print production   Larissa Frost,
                            Nigel Longuet
Thanks to: Mina Patria,
                            Tim Cook,
                            Caroline Hamilton,
                            Claire Clewley,
                            Jennifer Dixon.

Lonely Planet Offices

Australia

90 Maribyrnong St, Footscray, Victoria, 3011,
Australia
Phone: 03 8379 8000
Email: talk2us@lonelyplanet.com.au

USA

150 Linden St, Oakland, CA 94607
Phone: 510 250 6400
Email: info@lonelyplanet.com

United Kingdom

240 Blackfriars Road, London, SE1 8NW
Phone: 020 3771 5100
Email: go@lonelyplanet.co.uk

Published in September 2015 by Lonely Planet
Publications Pty Ltd
ABN 36 005 607 983
ISBN: 978 1 74360 772 5
www.lonelyplanetkids.com
© Lonely Planet 2015
© Photographs as indicated 2015
Printed in Singapore

HOW TO BE AN
INTERNATIONAL
SPY

ANDY BRIGGS

CONTENTS

SO YOU WANT TO BE TO A SPY?

Well it's going to involve a lot of tough preparation. Only the very best recruits can become fully fledged agents who we trust out in the field. However, if you think you have it in you, then get ready for some serious training.

SPIES LIKE US

In this book you will discover what it takes to be a spy. Learn the art of **SECRET CODES**, practise tailing people and building secret dossiers, discover amazing **GADGETS** and much more. At the end of some sections you will get a heads-up on **KEYWORDS** to remember and each step will elevate you from the rank of **RECRUIT** through to a full-blown **SECRET AGENT**.

To be a successful spy, you must first know what it is a spy actually does. Let's see what the dictionary says:

Definition of a **SPY**:

A spy works for a government or organization to secretly obtain information on an enemy or competitor. The professional term for spying is **ESPIONAGE**.

RIGHT NOW YOU
ARE RANKED AS A

RECRUIT

AND ONLY THE BEST GET
PROMOTED. GOOD LUCK!

TYPES OF SECRETS

Can you keep a secret? If you can't then you're going to have real trouble – it's one of the most important aspects of the job! The secrets you might be dealing with fall into three basic areas:

MILITARY SECRETS

Knowing how many troops the enemy has, where they are located and how well they are armed is vital to any country, especially in times of war. Knowing the strength of an enemy means you can find weak points or launch surprise attacks against them. But it's not just governments who try to discover such information; military secrets can also be used by terrorists to pick out targets and find their weaknesses.

INDUSTRIAL SECRETS

Imagine a technology company learning the secrets of a competitor months before they announce a new phone – then immediately launching their own version based on this stolen technology. Or a pharmaceutical company releasing a new drug before their rival, who spent many years developing it. This kind of industrial and corporate espionage really does happen!

POLITICAL SECRETS

From blackmailing politicians about their private lives through to discovering sensitive information about a country's economy, political secrets are just as valuable as technological ones. Imagine knowing how a government intends to act towards other countries – and even who they are spying on.

TYPES OF SPIES

MOLES

Moles are hidden deep within governments or organizations. As part of their job they will have access to secret files, although they won't usually steal these unless instructed to do so.

DOUBLE AGENTS

These sneaky spies often pretend to spy for one country, when in fact they are spying for another. For example, an American agent spying in Russia decides to pass false information back to America while actually passing on secret information to the Russians. The real skill of a double agent is creating and distributing disinformation – information that sounds real enough but is actually a lie.

SLEEPER AGENTS

Sleepers don't fall asleep on the job (never a wise move for any spy!). Instead, they work their way through the ranks of governments or other organizations, accessing secrets that would otherwise be almost impossible to get. Sleeper agents often don't spy for many years and are only activated when needed.

DEFECTORS

Sometimes you just don't agree with the boss and want to switch sides. That makes you a defector, and a very dangerous person at that. If you become a defector, you'll have to watch your back at all times.

SPIES IN HISTORY

You might have seen the glamour and adventure of spies through characters like James Bond and think that spycraft is a modern invention – but that's not the case. The art of spying is an ancient and respected one, occurring around the world and across many cultures. Spying has been used throughout history so that armies and governments could gain the upper hand.

ANCIENT EGYPT

The earliest recorded example of spying comes from ancient Egypt around 1274 BC. During the war between Pharaoh Ramesses and a group called the Hittites, spies were sent into the Egyptian camp, posing as deserting soldiers. They convinced the Egyptians that the enemy army was much further away than it really was. The cocky Pharaoh believed the spies and marched some of his men into an ambush.

SPIES IN THE BIBLE

The crafty Hittites weren't the only historical figures doing some shady spying, *The Old Testament* is littered with examples of espionage. One example from the *Book of Numbers* sees Moses sending out spies to check the land ahead when the Israelites reached the borders of Canaan.

THE ART OF WAR

Meanwhile, in ancient China, military general Sun Tzu spoke of how useful spies were in his famous book, *The Art of War* (a manual about how to conduct warfare, not paint it, in case you were confused).

Name:

JAMES ARMISTEAD LAFAYETTE

During the American Revolution, Lafayette became the first Afro-American double agent when he began spying on the British. Lafayette was a slave when war broke out and was (remarkably) granted permission to join the army. He then posed as a runaway slave and infiltrated British General Benedict Arnold's camp.

THE FRUMENTARII

In ancient Rome, you couldn't even trust the wheat collectors – the Roman equivalent of the tax man. While Rome didn't have an organized spying network, the wheat collectors, known as the Frumentarii, performed the same duties as the Secret Service. Because they had access to locals and native lands, Emperor Hadrian used them to sneakily gather intelligence.

A SPY OF WORDS

There are rumours that playwright William Shakespeare was a spy for England. The finger has also been pointed at the man who influenced Shakespeare – Christopher Marlowe.

While at university, Marlowe had several unexplained absences during which he claimed to be engaged in 'matters of benefit to his country'.

Some say his mysteriously early death was a cover for him to change identity, becoming William Shakespeare himself! If he was a spy, then he was a good one, leaving a trail of mystery that still hasn't been untangled.

THE GREAT GAME

In the mid 1830s the term 'The Great Game' was used to describe the increasing rivalry between Britain and Russia over the Central Asian region, although there was nothing fun about it. An intense bout of spying occurred between both sides until war broke out in Afghanistan. Sandwiched between India and Russia, it was an important strategic country to claim (sadly, this is still a reason for ongoing conflict there almost 200 years later).

THE GREAT WAR

Spying rose to a peak during World War I (1914–1918) and it became a particularly deadly game to play. When 11 German spies were caught in Britain, they were sentenced to death at the hands of the firing squad at the Tower of London.

During the war, espionage techniques became ever more daring and paranoia rippled through the public. Anything and everything was used to convey secret messages – loaves of bread, the whirling arms of a windmill and even steam locomotives, which spat out Morse code messages (see page 56 for more on Morse).

Paranoia peaked when two cats and a dog were spotted repeatedly crossing British trenches, leading officers to suspect that the animals had been planted by the enemy to relay messages!

The war was the start of spy tradecraft as we know it now; the very skills you are about to learn in order to complete your training.

Name:

MARGARETHA GEERTRUIDA ZELLE MACLEOD

Also known as: MATA HARI

Margaretha Geertruida Zelle MacLeod – better known as Mata Hari – was a Dutch exotic dancer who lived in Paris. She wooed Allied generals into revealing wartime secrets, which she then passed on to the Germans. When she was finally caught and arrested, she had to face the firing squad for her crimes.

Name:

LUDOVICO ZENDER

Also known as: THE SARDINE SPY

German secret agent, Ludovico Zender, traded canned fish to Peru. But hidden in his invoices for sardines were coded details of British shipping movements along the Scottish coast. He was caught in 1915 when the British authorities noticed that sardines were not in season in the winter. He was the last spy to be executed at the Tower of London.

WORLD WAR II

When war broke out again in 1939, intelligence agencies were ready. This was a time of great technological innovations for espionage – the most notable being Germany's Enigma Machine (see page 55).

One of the ingenious ways of sending secret communications during World War II was by using special agents called Code Talkers. They used obscure languages to pass on messages, and the more successful teams were America's Native Americans. As only a small amount of people could speak languages such as Navajo, they could confidently add a further code on top of that and no-one would be any the wiser. Hitler knew the Americans had used Code Talkers in the First World War, so he sent people to try to learn the obscure language, but it proved too difficult!

REAL SPIES

Name:

FREDERICK JOUBERT DUQUESNE

Also known as: The Black Panther

Duquesne was South African by birth and a German spy. He hated the British so much that he spied for Germany in both World Wars. He was supposedly responsible for the sinking of the HMS *Hampshire*, which killed famous British military leader Lord Kitchener.

During the war, the importance of keeping secrets was taught across the Allied countries, using slogans and posters like these:

LOOSE LIPS

Sink Ships

You never know who's on the wires!

BE CAREFUL WHAT YOU SAY

Name:

VIRGINIA HALL

Also known as: Artemis

Artemis was the German codename for American secret agent Virginia Hall. She volunteered to work for the SOE (Special Operations Executive) and headed into Vichy, France to help the French Resistance. After the war she successfully worked for the CIA. This would be an impressive record for anybody... but Artemis had one more surprise – she only had one leg!

THE COLD WAR

The Cold War between east and west perhaps best defines the world of spying as we know it. It all started after WWII, in approximately 1947, when a difference of opinion about politics split the Western Bloc (America and its NATO allies) and the Soviet Union (now called Russia) and its allies. These powerful countries became known as the 'Superpowers'.

It became known as the Cold War not because of the chilly winters, but because there was no actual fighting between the two sides. This was partly because both sides had a massive arsenal of nuclear weapons that would obliterate the enemy... and probably end all life on Earth. This became known as MAD, mostly because it was.

The Cold War fuelled the desire to get into space – and the Soviet Union led the way by sending both the first satellite (Sputnik 1) and first human (Yuri Gagarin) into orbit. This rush to exploit outer space led to an incredible development in the world of espionage: spy satellites armed with cameras able to photograph any spot on the planet!

The Cold War ended in 1991, after the collapse of the Soviet Union. This left the United States as the only remaining superpower.

REAL SPIES

REAL SPIES

Name:

THE ROSENBERGS

Two of the most infamous Soviet spies were Julius and Ethel Rosenberg, a married couple who passed secrets to the Soviet Union's KGB. Among the many secrets shared was the design of a weapon that was used to shoot down the U-2 in 1960. The Rosenbergs were finally caught and executed by electric chair – making them the only two American civilians to be executed for espionage during the entire Cold War.

Name:

OLEG GORDIEVSKY

Gordievsky was a KGB colonel who became a highly placed spy for the UK's MI6 and provided invaluable information during the Cold War. He was suddenly interrogated by his KGB superiors who became suspicious of his actions, although he was later released and kept under surveillance. Despite this he managed to send a communication to MI6 and a plan was launched to get him out of Russia. He now lives in London, and has written several books about spying!

KEYWORDS

SUPERPOWERS: The world was split into two superpowers – the United States and the Soviet Union. The USA included NATO (North Atlantic Treaty Organization), made up of (amongst others) UK, France, Germany, Spain, and Italy. The Soviet Union's allies included Poland, Czechoslovakia and Hungary.

MAD: 'Mutually Assured Destruction' is what stopped either superpower launching a nuclear war. The theory was that as soon as one side launched an attack, the other would almost immediately fight back with everything they had. The result would be the complete annihilation of both sides.

CONTROL: The general term given to the head spy who recruits and controls other spies, moles or informants (otherwise known as assets). They give instructions and gather the information so that their asset doesn't communicate with anybody else.

WHICH SIDE ARE YOU ON?

YOUR TRAINING STARTS NOW, AGENT! THERE IS NO GOING BACK.

Once you turn the next page you will have committed to begin your training as a spy.

The fast-paced world of international spying is one filled with a whole alphabet soup of secret agencies, and knowing your CIA from your MSS can be a matter of life and death! Luckily, the names of the international intelligence services are not secrets, so you can write down their names without having to use a code... although you will have to have a good memory!

To begin with you need to pick a side to work for. That usually depends on which country you live in – but the choice is yours. Once you have picked a side, then you will be able to form your own spy agency which will work for them. Let's take a look at some of the biggest intelligence agencies in the world. Choose wisely, Recruit. We don't want you ending up being a double or even a triple agent!

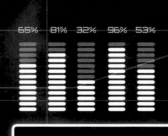

65%   81%   32%   96%   53%

DID YOU KNOW?

India's Intelligence Bureau (often simply called the IB) is supposedly the oldest in the world.

DID YOU KNOW?

Costa Rica is one of the few countries in the world not to have any military forces? The Vatican City is another. Although no army doesn't mean they don't have spies...

INTELLIGENCE TYPES

The world of intelligence gathering has categories. As an agent you are expected to know them all!

HUMINT: Human Intelligence, gathered by an agent making personal contacts and gathering information through trust – often risking their own lives.

SIGINT: Signal Intelligence, gathered by snooping in on regular communications between people. A technique known as COMINT is used for phone calls, whereas ELINT is used for electronic, satellite and radio communications.

GEOINT: Geospatial Intelligence. Gathered from unmanned aerial drones and satellite images.

MASINT: Measurement and Signals Intelligence. This involves analyzing sound, radiation and chemical emissions to work out what the enemy is trying to hide.

OSINT: Open Source Intelligence. This can be information easily found on the internet (from webpages to Facebook pages), published in magazines or books – or even codes to enemy agents hidden within letters pages of gossip magazines!

AGENCIES USUALLY COVER THREE AREAS:

DOMESTIC INTELLIGENCE – keeping an eye on potential threats in your own country.

FOREIGN INTELLIGENCE – dealing with the threats from international terrorist groups and aggressive foreign countries.

MILITARY INTELLIGENCE – providing specific information about an enemy's weapons, troops numbers, locations and battle plans.

ANSWER: Communications Intelligence and Electronic Intelligence.

TEST

Okay, Recruit, let's see if you've been paying attention. What are **COMINT** and **ELINT** abbreviations for? Use your spy skills now to try and decipher them!

SPYING IN THE USA

Welcome to the world of intelligence agencies. Let's take a look at one of the most famous to start us off – from its humble beginnings as the OSS, to becoming the global powerhouse of the CIA as we know it today.

1500
2500
3500
4500
5500
6500
7500
8500
9500
10500
11500

OSS

THE OFFICE OF STRATEGIC SERVICES

Formed: 13 June, 1942
Ended: 20 September, 1945
Type: Foreign Intelligence

You would expect the USA – the world's greatest superpower – to have impressive secret agencies... and it does, but it wasn't always this way. As World War II broke out across Europe, the US scrambled to combine its many independent agencies – that never really shared information – into one efficient organization. This became known as the OSS and it conducted and coordinated espionage operations behind enemy lines.

In January 1946, President Truman created the Central Intelligence Group (CIG), which then became, a year later (presumably because nobody liked the name), the Central Intelligence Agency, which still performs the same duties the OSS did.

CIA

THE CENTRAL INTELLIGENCE AGENCY

Formed: 18 September, 1947
Official website: www.cia.gov
Type: Foreign Intelligence

Welcome to the Farm! That's what agents call the CIA, not because cows run it, but because it is located in the lovely wooded countryside in the Langley neighbourhood of McLean, Virginia. Now, thanks to Hollywood, the CIA is the world's most famous secret organization!

The CIA is huge – employing approximately 21,500 people – although that figure is highly classified, so don't tell anybody! To keep their jobs, employees are expected to undergo a lie-detector test (known as a polygraph) every three years. Try not to fail yours... or else.

NSA

NATIONAL SECURITY AGENCY

Formed: 4 November, 1952
Official website: www.nsa.gov
Type: Foreign Intelligence

Every text message you send, every email you write and every conversation you have over the phone – even if you whisper it – will probably pass through the NSA's computers.

Based in Fort Meade, Maryland, the NSA is in charge of America's SIGINT by using amazingly hi-tech methods to intercept telephone, satellite, internet and radio communications as well as bugging targets to overhear absolutely everything.

Little was known about the NSA's shadowy operations until Edward Snowden illegally leaked documents demonstrating that the agency intercepts the communications of over a billion people worldwide, including world leaders such as German Chancellor, Angela Merkel, and probably you and your parents too.

Imagery ©2015 Google, Map data ©2015 Google

NATIONAL SECURITY AGENCY · UNITED STATES OF AMERICA

FORT MEADE

LANGLEY

REAL SPIES

Name:

EDWARD SNOWDEN

In 2013, NSA analyst Edward Snowden leaked lots of classified information from the NSA. He went on the run, releasing some of the files to the media and exposing the massive scale of the NSA's operations. Snowden fled to Hong Kong, then to Moscow where he was offered asylum. Snowden claims he betrayed the secrets because people needed to know the full extent of the NSA's power; but others believe he was an unwilling mole played by the Russians.

ARE YOU SAD?

The Special Activities Division (SAD) of the CIA is where the fun really begins, with agents employed in covert activities behind enemy lines. This comes in two flavours:

SOG: Special Operations Group. These are deep-cover spies who seek out information from behind enemy lines. Agents never carry anything that will link them to the CIA. If you're caught, then the CIA will claim they've never heard of you!

PAG: Political Action Group. PAG operatives specialize in such warfare methods as persuading people to change their opinions or influence news stories, sabotaging the enemy's banks and conducting online attacks.

PSYWAR

Music is regularly used in psychological warfare. In 1989 the USA invaded Panama to stop dictator General Noriega. The dictator hid in an embassy, which was then surrounded by speakers and bombarded 24/7 by loud music until he eventually surrendered. So the next time your parents ask you to turn your music down, it might be because they think you're conducting **PSYWAR** on them...

MOBILE SPIES

The NSA can intercept mobile communications no matter where in the world you are. Plus, their sophisticated software can activate your phone's GPS and tell them your exact location, so hiding under the bed to make a phone call is not going to help.

Clever spies will deactivate their phone's GPS, but if the NSA really needs to find them they use a method called **TRIANGULATION**.

The telephone companies know which mobile tower the spy is connected to and which others are close by. Knowing the three towers' locations will betray the spy's approximate position!

Even if your mobile phone is *switched off* it can still be reached, and the camera and microphone remotely activated!

THE BLACK CHAMBER

Before the NSA, and even before the OSS, the Cipher Bureau – also known as the Black Chamber – became the United States' first codebreaking unit after World War I. It intercepted communications and was, basically, reading people's letters. In 1929 the Black Chamber was closed by the Secretary of State, who later said: 'Gentlemen do not read each other's mail'.

SERVING CELL

RX1+1A

Cell ID 1

RX2

Cell ID 2

RX3

Cell ID 3

TRIANGULATED LOCATION

KEYWORDS

CRYPTANALYSIS: decoding a message without knowing the key to doing so. You'll be trained up in this later!

TRADECRAFT: the techniques used by spies. You'll discover more Tradecraft secrets as we progress with your training.

AND THE OTHERS...

While the CIA and NSA are the better-known top-secret organizations across the United States, there are a total of 17 intelligence gathering agencies that are always on the look out for new agents! Among them are:

FBI

THE FEDERAL BUREAU OF INVESTIGATION

Formed: 26 July, 1908
Official website: www.FBI.gov
Type: Law Enforcement

This is where the G-men (and women) live. The FBI is charged with tackling criminal activity within the United States, or against its citizens around the globe. While they don't 'spy' in the traditional sense, the FBI employs agents who work undercover within criminal organizations.

In case you're wondering, 'G-men' was a term used in the 1920s by gangsters like Al Capone and is short for 'Government-men'.

Imagery ©2015 Google, Map data ©2015 Google

DIA

THE DEFENSE INTELLIGENCE AGENCY

Formed: 1 October, 1961
Official website: www.dia.mil
Type: Military Intelligence

The DIA is America's main military intelligence organization and does very similar work to the CIA in collecting information that relates to the security of America from military threats. In times of war, the DIA is responsible for letting the President know what is going on. While they commonly use HUMINT to dig out secrets, they specialize in MASINT.

While the DIA has its own headquarters in Washington DC, they run most of their operations from within the Department of Defense's huge Pentagon building.

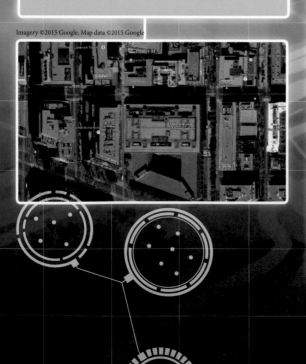
Imagery ©2015 Google, Map data ©2015 Google

Name:

J EDGAR HOOVER

Hoover started in the Bureau of Investigation, but helped to found the FBI, turning it into one of the world's leading crime-fighting organizations.

He insisted the FBI keep files on a number of high-profile people, including celebrities, such as Charlie Chaplin who was, at the time, the world's biggest movie star – and a suspected communist spy.

65%

THE PENTAGON

This building is perhaps the most famous secret HQ on the planet – and it's not exactly hard to find! Located within Washington DC, it belongs to the Department of Defense and contains units from all of America's armed services.

The five-sided building is most deserving of its name. It is constructed with five separate rings, and the security increases the closer you move to the centre. It has five floors (with an extra two basement levels) and over 27 kilometres (17 miles) of corridor!

NGA

NATIONAL GEOSPATIAL-INTELLIGENCE AGENCY

Imagery ©2015 Google, Map data ©2015 Google

Formed: 1996
Official website: www.nga.mil
Type: Military Intelligence

The NGA probably wins the 'coolest office to work in' award. Clocking in as the third largest building in Washington DC, its headquarters in Virginia boasts an atrium so large that it could house the Statue of Liberty!

The NGA collects and analyzes GEOINT, distributing it to the other agencies when they need it. They also support combat situations, with satellites providing live feeds of the action all the way from outer space! You'll learn more about the incredible capabilities of these satellites later in your training.

EYES IN THE SKY

Spying doesn't always have to be completely secret, and it can sometimes provide assistance in dire circumstances, as well as having some unexpected benefits. After Hurricane Katrina struck America in 2005, NGA provided aerial pictures of the affected areas in order to help rescue services reach them quickly. During several Olympic games, the NGA got to watch the event from directly above, as well as helping out the local security services. Remember, every time you log onto Google Maps, those images have been supplied by the NGA, allowing you to spy from your armchair!

NRO

NATIONAL RECONNAISSANCE OFFICE

Formed: 1961
Official website: www.nro.gov
Type: Foreign Intelligence

Although this agency has been around since 1961, its existence was only made official by the US Government in 1992.

Their motto is 'vigilance from above'. The NRO designs, builds and operates the satellites that are used by every other agency. They boast that they provide eyes and ears in places no agent can venture...

And it's true. If you walk in your garden, put this book on the ground and stand up, can you still read the text? An NRO satellite can – and that's in orbit at least 960km (600mi) above your head! They can even allegedly track submarines in the deepest oceans...

SPYING IN THE UK

MI5

MILITARY INTELLIGENCE: SECTION 5

Formed: 1909
Official website: www.mi5.gov.uk
Type: Domestic Intelligence

This agency is officially called the Security Service (SS) – but it's more commonly known as MI5. However, a slang term commonly used is Thames House (the name of the HQ building... which sits on the River Thames. Nobody said spies had good imaginations!).

MI5 looks after the United Kingdom's internal safety. Just before the outbreak of WWI, the Secret Service Bureau became MI5. It was officially renamed the Security Service in 1931.

The agency became involved in fighting terrorism on the UK's shores and in recent years they have also helped the police fight serious crime across the country. It was discovered that MI5 keeps files on 272,000 people in the UK. Think about it another way – in a packed crowd in Wembley stadium, MI5 would have a file on at least 562 people!

Imagery ©2015 Google. Map data ©2015 Google

NICKNAME

Today, MI5 is still known by the country's civil servants as Box 500. This comes from the PO Box address used during WWII. Despite changing addresses, the old nickname continues to stick.

65% 81% 32% 96% 53%

MI6

MILITARY INTELLIGENCE: SECTION 6

Formed: 1909
Official website: www.sis.gov.uk
Type: Foreign Intelligence

MI6 is one of the more famous secret agencies in the world – all thanks to the fictional spy, James Bond.

MI6's official name is the Secret Intelligence Service (SIS) and its existence was never officially confirmed until 1994. Before that, the huge beige and green building in the heart of London was a complete secret!

Through the two World Wars and the frosty Cold War, MI6 provided vital intelligence for the UK and its allies.

These days, MI6 is one of the leading organizations fighting terrorism around the globe.

LONDON

REAL SPIES

Name:

IAN LANCASTER FLEMING

Ian Lancaster Fleming is best known as the creator of the fictional spy, James Bond. Bond was inspired by Fleming's own adventures during WWII as a naval intelligence officer who embarked on thrilling adventures behind enemy lines.

Name:

DAVID JOHN MOORE CORNWALL

It seems that spies make excellent authors. David John Moore Cornwell, former MI6 employee, wrote a series of bestselling spy books under the more famous pen name: John le Carré.

BLETCHLEY PARK

The grounds of this beautiful manor house, nestled in the English countryside, was home to some of the smartest mathematicians and puzzle solvers of WWII. Their work at cracking enemy codes is credited to have shortened the war by as much as two to four years! The information obtained here was so sensitive that 'Top Secret' was not a strong enough classification and a new term had to be created: 'Ultra'.

Codebreakers originally worked in Huts – for example Hut 4 was Naval Intelligence, Hut 10 was for MI6 and Hut 2 was where you could drink tea and beer.

GCHQ

GOVERNMENT COMMUNICATIONS HEADQUARTERS

Formed: 1919
Official website: www.gchq.gov.uk
Type: Foreign Intelligence

In the middle of the English town of Cheltenham is a flying saucer – at least that's what it looks like from the air. This is the headquarters of GCHQ – the British version of America's NSA. Like the NSA, they snoop in on phone calls, emails and internet traffic.

GCHQ is made up from two secret units: the Composite Signals Organisation (CSO), which gathers the UK's SIGINT; and the Communications-Electronics Security Group (CESG), which secures the country's cyber network from hackers who are up to no good.

SPYING IN RUSSIA

KGB

KOMITET GOSUDARSTVENNOY BEZOPASNOSTI

Formed: 13 March, 1954
Ended: 3 December, 1991
Type: Foreign & Domestic Intelligence

During the Soviet-era the KGB was the great Cold War rival to the CIA. It originally started as a secret police organization called Cheka, but was soon combined with other departments to form the mighty KGB.

During the existence of the USSR (see page 35), it was responsible for guarding the Soviet Union's vast borders, watching over politicians, and stopping anti-communist activities – as well as spying on the USSR's enemies!

Imagery ©2015 DigitalGlobe, Map data ©2015 Google

MOSCOW

REAL SPIES

Name:

VLADIMIR PUTIN

Vladimir Putin has been the President of Russia on two separate occasions (2000–2008 and again from 2012). He started his career as a KGB agent in East Germany, using his fluent German to recruit foreigners as spies for Russia while undercover as a translator.

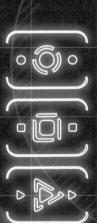

FSB

FEDERALNAYA SLUZHBA BEZOPASNOSTI ROSSIYSKOY FEDERATSII

Formed: 12 April, 1996
Official website: www.fsb.ru
Type: Domestic Intelligence

The Cold War ended when the communist system of government collapsed in Russia, finally giving more freedom to its population. With the end of the Cold War the KGB became the FSB (translated as the Federal Security Service of the Russian Federation).

The FSB is modern Russia's main security agency, responsible for domestic intelligence – Russia's equivalent of MI5.

For the security of Russia's colossal borders, the FSB operates a separate department called the FPS (Federal Border Guard Service). Protecting these borders is a mammoth task. Until you look at a map, it's difficult to imagine that Russia has land borders on the west with Finland and Ukraine – while eastwards it has sea borders with Japan and America!

The FSB rapidly gained a reputation as one of the best intelligence agencies in the world as they cracked down on the threat of terrorism. They were so effective that Russia was named 'the worst place to be a terrorist' – which is a huge compliment!

65% 81% 32% 96% 53%

65%

SVR

SLUZHBA VNESHNEY RAZVEDKI

Formed: December, 1991
Official website: www.svr.gov.ru
Type: Foreign Intelligence

Imagery ©2015 DigitalGlobe, Map data ©2015 Google

The SVR is Russia's Foreign Intelligence Service, working closely with the FSB. Outside of Russia, the SVR shares intelligence with allies, including sending counter-terrorism information around the globe. They're also responsible for providing protection to Russian ministers and employees who live overseas.

Like every other country's Foreign Intelligence service, the SVR actively recruits agents and moles who live abroad.

If you choose to work for the SVR then get ready for one of the most intensive training programs of any intelligence organization... and be prepared never to speak about it!

Name:

ANNA CHAPMAN

Anna Chapman hit the headlines when she pleaded guilty to being a Russian sleeper agent in 2010.

After she was deported back to Russia it was revealed that she wasn't a very good spy – her phone was registered to the address: 99 Fake Street!

WHAT WAS THE USSR?

Between 1922 and 1991 Russia and several Eastern Bloc countries were known as the Union of Soviet Socialist Republics, shortened to the Soviet Union, or the USSR. As a communist country, their beliefs fuelled the Cold War against the West, which led to the development of many of the spying techniques still in use today.

MSS

MINISTRY OF STATE SECURITY

Formed: July, 1983
Official website: NONE
Type: Foreign Intelligence

Little is known about the Ministry of State Security of the People's Republic of China (MSS) but if you wish to join this mysterious organization then you will become one of the many agents that are thought to be hiding in plain sight amongst the world's Chinese community and businesses.

Aside from obtaining foreign intelligence, the MSS monitors and censors the internet pages that can be seen in China, as access to information about the outside world is strictly controlled.

China is at the forefront of cyber-spying and has been blamed for GHOSTNET, a huge online operation that targeted non-Chinese government computers around the globe. Of course, like all great spies, China has denied being involved...

Imagery ©2015 DigitalGlobe, Map data ©2015 AutoNavi, Google

REAL SPIES

Name:

LARRY WU-TAI CHIN

Perhaps one of the most prolific Chinese spies caught in America, Chin was originally recruited in 1948. He worked as a translator for the CIA, and sold sensitive secrets to China for decades. He was finally caught and convicted in 1986.

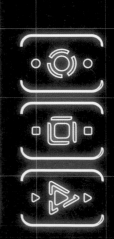

TITAN RAIN

One of the most effective computer hacks ever was dubbed TITAN RAIN, which was a series of advanced hacks on American and British computers starting in 2003.

Targets included sensitive information from aerospace companies and NASA. Of course, China never admitted to the attacks - but the actions caused distrust between the US and China for years.

65% 81% 32% 96% 53%

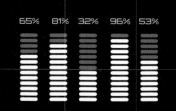

SPYING IN ISRAEL

THE MOSSAD

Formed: 13 December, 1949
Official website:
www.mossad.gov.il
Type: Foreign Intelligence

The Mossad is Israel's formidable intelligence gathering agency. It is so secretive that the public does not know its exact location, although people within the intelligence community often refer to it as Glilot Junction, referring to the highway allegedly close by.

Another term the Mossad is known by is The Institute, referring to the direct translation of the name from Hebrew.

The Mossad performs the same role as other global intelligence agencies, however it has another unique function: to protect Jewish communities around the world and bring Jews to Israel for safety should they require it. An example of this was seen in 1984 when the Mossad conducted *Operation Moses* to evacuate Ethiopian Jews from the hardships of famine.

TEL AVIV

KIDONS

Within the Mossad lies a shadowy team of agents known as **KIDONS**. They are specialized at infiltrating behind enemy lines and skilled in the art of assassination. Very little is known about this elite group, but they are thought to be responsible for *Operation Wrath of God*, which assassinated those responsible for killing 11 members of the Israeli Olympic team during the notorious 1972 Munich Olympic Games.

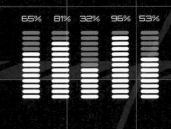

AMAN

DIRECTORATE OF MILITARY INTELLIGENCE

Formed: 1950
Official website: NONE
Type: Military Intelligence

Agents who want to be in AMAN have to be exceptionally tough and smart. Applicants must undergo the rigorous Havatzalot Program – strenuous physical field training – and learn cutting-edge tradecraft. If that wasn't enough, applicants must also complete a degree in Middle Eastern studies.

Out of the thousands of people who apply every year only 25 are accepted onto one of the toughest courses in any intelligence agency. There are thought to be about 7,000 employees.

There are several departments within AMAN, all with very different roles that are normally assigned to separate agencies. For example, the Foreign Relations Department looks after the safety of Israeli ambassadors abroad as well as working with other foreign intelligence services.

It has a naval and air force intelligence unit that can operate independently and is also responsible for Israel's huge drone program. You'll learn more about drones as you complete more stages of your training. Patience is a virtue, Recruit!

DGSE

DIRECTION
GÉNÉRALE
DE LA SÉCURITÉ
EXTÉRIEURE

Formed: 2 April, 1982
Official website: www.defense.gouv.fr
/english/dgse
Type: Foreign Intelligence

If you wish to be recruited into the ranks of DGSE, then you will be part of France's main foreign intelligence agency.

One of the more intriguing divisions within the agency is the 'Division Action'. Aside from planning operations behind enemy lines, the division also tests security of the country's own submarine bases, airports and nuclear plants by attempting to break in!

Their headquarters are known as CAT (Centre Administratif des Tourelles), located in Paris. The DGSE are capable of intercepting any mobile phone call, even in the underground Metro, instantly and without a warrant.

Imagery ©2015 Google, Map data ©2015 Google

FRENCH RESISTANCE

Perhaps the most famous French secret agents were the Resistance who fought against Germany's occupation during WWII. They risked their lives fighting the enemy and gathered priceless intelligence to pass on to the Allies.

Imagery ©2015 Google, Map data ©2015 Google

DGSI

DIRECTION GÉNÉRALE DE LA SÉCURITÉ INTÉRIEURE -

Formed: 12 May 2014
Official website: NONE
Type: Domestic Intelligence

Welcome to France's equivalent of MI5, this young organization recently replaced the DCRI (Direction Centrale du Renseignement Intérieur), becoming part of France's Homeland Security.

Although the DGSI deals with intelligence, it really doesn't like people talking about what it does. Back when it was known as DCRI, it was so secretive that in 2013 they insisted that an article about them was taken off the French Wikipedia website.

PARIS

65% 81% 32% 96% 53%

REAL SPIES

Name:

ANDRÉE PEEL

Also known as: AGENT ROSE

One of the most famous Resistance heroes was Agent Rose – whose real name was Andrée Peel. Despite spending time in two Nazi concentration camps, she was responsible for saving the lives of over 100 Allied pilots.

FIVE EYES – FVEY

Even for a super-secret agent, it's good to share sometimes! Of course, you need to be totally sure that you trust the person you're talking to, and that they're on the same side as you. Thankfully, FVEY have that covered!

Since WWII, Allied countries have shared their foreign intelligence on their mutual enemies. Five Eyes, known as FVEY, is a pact between the United States, Canada, United Kingdom, New Zealand and Australia ensuring vital intelligence is passed safely between them. As well as being allies, the shared language is a huge help in guaranteeing that intelligence is not wrongly translated. You don't want your message: 'I have located the nuclear warhead' to be translated into Japanese as: 'I will have my mother's baguette for super happy fish golf'.

FVEY may be about helping each other out, but it also serves a more sinister purpose...

Within each of the Allied countries it is illegal to collect information about their own citizens – however, there is nothing stopping them asking a friend for help.

So, if GCHQ wanted to intercept the calls and emails of a target in London, all they had to do was call their pals in America's NSA and ask them to spy – because, to the NSA, a target in London counts as foreign intelligence!

STONEGHOST

The internet we know is only a tiny part of the global internet. One of these inaccessible areas is the shadowy top-secret network of Stoneghost – the computer network controlled by America's DIA, that links the FVEY members together so they can freely share intelligence.

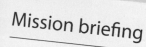

Mission briefing

Now you know about the big world of secret agencies, start to think about what skills you can develop to become the ultimate spy. Perhaps you are athletic and will make a terrific **FIELD AGENT**, tailing people – or more of a puzzle solver better suited to **CODE BREAKING**? Over the next chapters you will hone your skills to become a secret agent any agency would be proud of.

OK Recruit, the hard work starts here. You need to start looking and acting like a real spy, so we're going to begin SPY CAMP!

CLASSIFIED

Don't forget, everything you're about to learn is TOP SECRET! Good luck! And be warned – this chapter may self-destruct when you have finished reading...

CLASSIFIED

UNCLASSIFIED

Basically anything you don't mind other people knowing. It could be instructions on how to use the toaster, through to information about the weather.

SECRET

This is straightforward information that you don't want anybody to know about outside a certain group of people. Governments and organizations consider that such information would cause serious damage if it were leaked.

RESTRICTED

This means that there are certain people you won't want to have access to the information. For example, you might not want instructions about when you are having a party to fall in the hands of certain people... such as your parents! This is also sometimes called **CONFIDENTIAL**, **PRIVATE** or **EYES ONLY**.

SECURITY CLEARANCE

Every country has its own terms for the different level of security given to the information that's flying around, but they generally follow this scale of secrecy:

OFFICIAL

This will be information you don't want anybody outside your company or government department knowing before it is cleared by the boss. So an OFFICIAL school letter might tell you it's a snow day and you can have the day off, and you'll know your head teacher has said it's ok – woo-hoo!

TOP SECRET

The highest level of secrecy. This could include vital information about weapons and future plans. Governments and organizations consider that such information would cause terrible damage if it were leaked.

NATIONAL SECURITY

This lies at the heart of all spying activity – the security of the nation (or in some cases, the company) you work for. It's a favourite term used by agents and cops who quickly want to shut people up when they are asking awkward questions: 'Sorry, Ma'am – it's a National Security situation.'

COMPARTMENTALIZED INFORMATION

This is an extra layer of security. Something may be marked SECRET, but if it is compartmentalized then only people who directly need to access it are allowed to see it. Think of the compartments as rooms. If everybody in your house had Secret clearance, only those within individual rooms would have access to specific compartmentalized information.

NATO uses its own variations: **NATO RESTRICTED**, **NATO CONFIDENTIAL**, **NATO SECRET** and the amazing-sounding **COSMIC TOP SECRET**.

CODE NAMES

There's no point in being a spy if you're going to use your real name, which is why James Bond really wouldn't be that successful in the real world. This double identity is how spies live their lives.

Code names can be anything. You could spell your name backwards – so Andy becomes Ydna – although it wouldn't take a rocket scientist to work out your real name. And if you're called Bob or Anna then you are in real trouble.

The best code names are ones that can't be directly linked to you and is something you will be comfortable using throughout your spying career, without changing.

A	RED	N	WOBBLY
B	HOWLING	O	INFINITE
C	MIDNIGHT	P	STORM
D	SILVER	Q	RACING
E	AMBER	R	PHANTOM
F	DARK	S	SONIC
G	FURIOUS	T	DIGITAL
H	FLAMING	U	ELECTRIC
I	SMELLY	V	WHITE
J	HUMUNGOUS	W	BIONIC
K	AWESOME	X	AMAZING
L	FROZEN	Y	ANGRY
M	INVISIBLE	Z	JUGGLING

If you're struggling to come up with something that's right for you, use our code-name generator to help you. Find the first letter of your first name in the box above – that's your new first name. Then select your birth month from the box opposite. Voilà! There's your new last name.

JANUARY	SHARK
FEBRUARY	CYCLONE
MARCH	SHADOW
APRIL	CLAW
MAY	FALCON
JUNE	DOLPHIN
JULY	STAR
AUGUST	SQUIRREL
SEPTEMBER	TORNADO
OCTOBER	GRASSHOPPER
NOVEMBER	EAGLE
DECEMBER	PULSAR

FAMOUS CODE NAMES

OPERATION OVERLORD – the code name given for the Allied invasion of Normandy during WWII.

MANHATTAN PROJECT – the code name given to the American project that developed the nuclear bomb during WWII.

TANK – oddly, this was the code name given to making the very first tank in WWI. The name stuck and became both the word and code name for the vehicle itself.

It's not just secret weapons and people who get assigned codes. **BLUE HARVEST** was the code name given to the film *Star Wars: Return of the Jedi*, just so the fans wouldn't know what was being filmed. **GROUP HUG** was the code name given to *The Avengers*.

Mission briefing

Come up with your own code name – something that you feel comfortable with, as you will be signing all your Top Secret documents with this.

Take your time. You will be known by this code name throughout the rest of your training, so it's important to get it right.

BUILD YOUR OWN HQ

As a spy you need somewhere to relax – a base to store the intelligence you've gathered and from which to plan your next mission. For this you will need a **HEADQUARTERS**. It has to be somewhere safe, away from prying eyes and defendable against your enemies – everybody else who doesn't have the same security clearance as you!

HOT HEADQUARTERS

THULE AIR BASE How's this for some icy inspiration? This US military installation lies within the Arctic Circle and, due to the weather, it is only accessible for three months per year.

AREA 51 This huge base is located north of Las Vegas bordered by the Extraterrestrial Highway. It's the United States' most secure military installation and, officially, it doesn't exist! It is where stealth fighters first flew and where it is thought future spy aircraft are built and tested.

Mission briefing

You may not be able to build an underground secret base, but you need to find a location in which you can construct your own HQ. It could be in your house – try the attic, the cellar or even under the stairs. If you have a garden, then maybe you can repurpose the shed or build a den from which you can tackle your training missions.

REMEMBER: your HQ is the one place you need to keep secret. Good luck, Recruit!

CHEYENNE MOUNTAIN America's Air Force Space Command runs perhaps the most famous underground base. Protected by a 25-ton door, built on huge springs to absorb the blasts and carved from solid granite, Cheyenne Mountain might not be so secret but it is invincible.

RAVEN ROCK Also known as Site R, this underground facility is used for the 'Continuity of Operations Plan' – a secret plan for how the USA would continue in the event of a cataclysm, such as a meteor strike or nuclear war.

SECURITY MEASURES

Later we will be looking at the gadgets you can create for defending your HQ, but here are some basic precautions you can take to safeguard your secrets and ensure that you can tell if anybody has been snooping around your secret stash.

HAIR TRIPWIRE

Pull out a hair, preferably from your own head. Give it a lick and carefully place it across the top of a drawer. If it's not there when you return, somebody has been snooping!

BACKSTOP

Slide a piece of paper part way under the door. Place a deodorant can on the paper. Leave the room and slowly close the door behind you, pulling the paper as you do, so that the can is directly behind the door. Carefully remove the paper. You will know if a spy has entered your HQ if the can has moved when you return.

FLOUR TRAIL

This only really works well on wooden or stone floors, otherwise you will end up with a complete mess! Sprinkle some flour at the entrance to your HQ as you leave. When a spy blunders in they will leave a trail of messy footprints! With any luck, you can follow the culprit's trail to discover who it was.

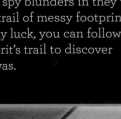

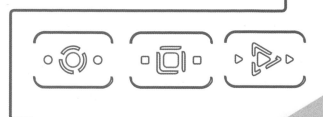

PENCIL BOMB

Take a handful of pencils and wrap an elastic band around the middle of them to keep them together. Grip half the pencils and twist clockwise a couple of times. Each twist will increase the tension – don't let go! Wedge the pencil bomb behind a cupboard door ensuring the door stops the pencil bomb from spinning. Once the snoop opens the door the two halves of the pencil-bomb will be free to spin rapidly – scaring off your intruder!

UNDERGROUND STASH

Loose floorboards and air conditioning vents are great places to hide secret documents from the eyes of prying spies.

NOT HERE!

Don't go hiding top-secret documents under your mattress because that is usually the first place people look!

51

NONE SHALL PASS!

Passwords aren't just for computers (you'll learn more about these later in your training), they are a tried and tested method of detecting if a friend or foe is trying to gain access to your HQ.

One of the most famous passwords comes from *Ali Baba and the Forty Thieves*: 'open sesame!'. This magical password opened a cave leading to great treasure.

During the Cold War, agents would creep up to one another in parks and say things like: 'The swan flies south in the winter,' then they would eagerly await the countersign: 'But they only eat fish in the summer,' which confirmed they were working on the same side!

If ever you have to work together with another agent or group of agents on a mission, it will be useful to assign passwords to each other. Don't forget to change them regularly, just in case the enemy has discovered the password. A good trick is to have a different password depending on which day it is. The more un-guessable the password, the better! Here are some silly examples you could try:

	PASSWORD	COUNTERSIGN
MONDAY	GOOD GRAVY	NEEDS MORE SALT
TUESDAY	CHILLY DAY	ONLY ON MARS
WEDNESDAY	IS THAT A CAT?	NO, IT'S A BADGER
THURSDAY	I'VE LOST MY HAT	IT IS IN NORWAY
FRIDAY	FISH?	NO, TUNA
SATURDAY	HAVE YOU SEEN MY DOG?	LAST THURSDAY
SUNDAY	BLESS YOU	A-CHOO!

FAMOUS PASSWORDS

00000000 – the Presidential password to launch a nuclear missile attack during the Cold War.

BUDDY – former US President Bill Clinton signed important electronic documents using this password. It was the name of his dog.

CHUCK NORRIS – the legendary actor's name was allegedly the password that would allow access to any Facebook account. Sadly, it no longer works.

SWORDFISH – originally used in an old Groucho Marx film as a password. It has lived on through history, reappearing in many films, and games as the password of choice.

OKAY AGENT – NOW YOU ARE UP AND RUNNING.

YOU ARE NO LONGER A RECRUIT.

YOU HAVE BEEN PROMOTED TO

CADET

AS A CADET YOUR SECURITY LEVEL HAS INCREASED, SO WE CAN NOW LET YOU INTO MORE SECRETS OF SPYCRAFT...

GET READY FOR SOME CODE BREAKING!

Okay, Cadet, now you have your HQ you need to start spying and reporting your findings. Simply writing this down won't do, no matter how secure your base is – you will have to learn how to write in secret codes!

KEEP YOUR EYE OUT, CODES CAN BE ANYWHERE...

The creation and breaking of codes is known as CRYPTANALYSIS from the Greek *kryptós* (hidden) and *analýein* (to untie). This usually involves a lot of maths, but also a good deal of logical thinking and common sense, so if you don't like maths then don't panic, all is not lost!

CAESAR'S CIPHER

This is one of the most basic methods of coding information and was used by the Roman General Julius Caesar. Write the alphabet down, then another version underneath – shifting each letter one step left or right:

ABCDEFGHIJKLMNOPQRSTUVWXYZ
BCDEFGHIJKLMNOPQRSTUVWXYZA

So now the word ENIGMA becomes FOJHNB.

This is known as a **SUBSTITUTION CIPHER**. The alphabet can be shifted as many steps as you want to make it harder to crack (Caesar shifted his alphabet by three letters).

One trick to help you break the code faster is to look at sentences which contain two-letter words. These may be common words, such as TO, AT, GO, OF – for example:

HP UP CFE

There are two two-letter words that end in the same letter – these should be easier to crack! TO and GO both end in 'O' - so the coded words could be TO and GO. Can you work out what the third word in this code is?

THE ENIGMA MACHINE

The most legendary 'unbreakable' code to come out of World War II was created by Nazi Germany's Enigma Machine.

It was quite complicated, but essentially worked by four rotors, marked with the alphabet, that were electronically turned as the message was typed – a simple **SUBSTITUTION CIPHER**. This could easily be broken – but each rotor could be set to 26 different positions to begin with (one for each letter of the alphabet). Further advancements in the design – such as stepping the rotors a letter ahead or behind – made the codes even more difficult to break.

Polish codebreakers were at the forefront of breaking the ever-more complex codes. Code breakers, based in Bletchley Park, were able to fully break the codes when they obtained a working Enigma Machine. Their work was so top secret that it was classified 'Ultra'. These broken codes were considered so valuable that Winston Churchill claimed: 'It was thanks to Ultra that we won the war.'

Mission briefing

Control has intercepted this substitution cipher – but they don't know how many steps the alphabet has shifted.

Can you break the code?
Clue: We're feeling rather peckish!

XAZQXK BXOZQF TC TME DGZ AGF AR EZMOWE!

COMMON CODES

Even though some codes may have been used for a long time, the general public are only familiar with their names, not how they work. The following codes should become basic knowledge to a Cadet like you!

MORSE CODE

This is **INTERNATIONAL MORSE CODE** – a rapid way of sending messages a letter or number at a time using light or sound. It's basically made up of **DOTS** and **DASHES**. This is achieved by flashing a light quickly for a **DOT** and slower for a **DASH**.

The same for audio tones - a quick **BEEP** is a **DOT**, a longer **BEEEEP** a **DASH**.

Codes are measured in **DOTS** (three **DOTS** make a **DASH**). When sending a message make sure that the pace of your code is steady.

A ●▬	Q ▬▬●▬	? ●●▬▬●●
B ▬●●●	R ●▬●	! ●●▬▬●▬
C ▬●▬●	S ●●●	: ▬▬▬●●●
D ▬●●	T ▬	" ●▬●●▬●
E ●	U ●●▬	' ●▬▬▬▬●
F ●●▬●	V ●●●▬	= ▬●●●▬
G ▬▬●	W ●▬▬	0 ▬▬▬▬▬
H ●●●●	X ▬●●▬	1 ●▬▬▬▬
I ●●	Y ▬●▬▬	2 ●●▬▬▬
J ●▬▬▬	Z ▬▬●●	3 ●●●▬▬
K ▬●▬	Ä ●▬●▬	4 ●●●●▬
L ●▬●●	Ö ▬▬▬●	5 ●●●●●
M ▬▬	Ü ●●▬▬	6 ▬●●●●
N ▬●	Ch ▬▬▬▬	7 ▬▬●●●
O ▬▬▬	. ●▬●▬●▬	8 ▬▬▬●●
P ●▬▬●	, ▬▬●●▬▬	9 ▬▬▬▬●

THE MOST IMPORTANT MORSE CODE TO REMEMBER IS: ●●● ▬▬▬ ●●●
THE INTERNATIONAL SIGN OF DISTRESS: SOS.

SEMAPHORE

Semaphore is a visual coding system traditionally shown using flags, although you can use a pair of torches, mirrors, your own arms or even a clock! The position of each 'flag' indicates a letter and, by simply moving position you can communicate codes over distance. Along with Morse code, this was one of the most widely used code systems at sea.

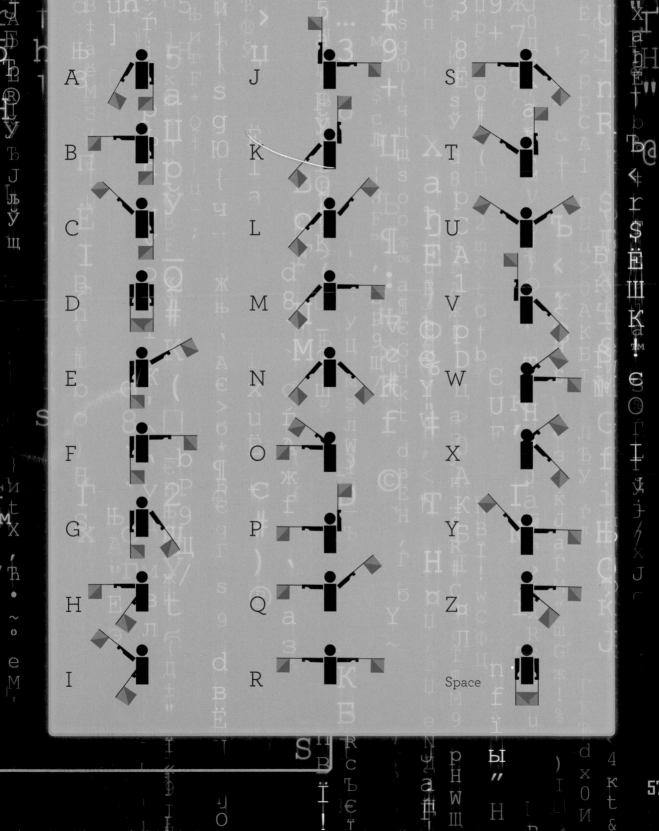

A

B

C

D

E

F

G

H

I

J

K

L

M

N

O

P

Q

R

S

T

U

V

W

X

Y

Z

Space

57

PIGPEN CIPHER

This old code is sometimes known as the Masonic cipher and can be split up in numerous ways – which makes it quite difficult to crack if you don't know how the code is split up in the first place.

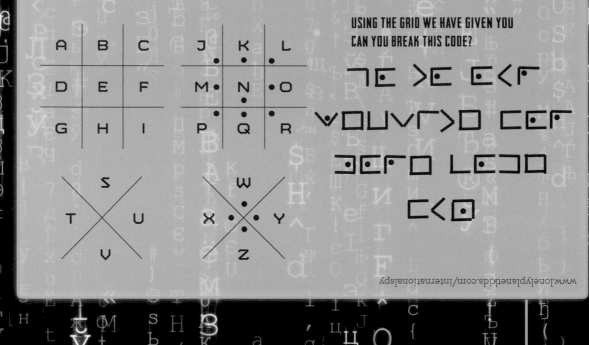

POLYBIUS CODE

The ancient Greek historian, Polybius, created another simple but very effective code. The letters of the alphabet are placed in a Polybius square:

	1	2	3	4	5
1	A	B	C	D	E
2	F	G	H	I/J	K
3	L	M	N	O	P
4	Q	R	S	T	U
5	V	W	X	Y	Z

In case you're wondering why I and J share the same square, Polybius' Greek alphabet only had 24 letters! Now read the numbers down then across to select the letter you want. So

A = 11   Y = 54
B = 12   Z = 55
C = 13

Can you crack it? 23 11 51 24 33 22   21 45 33,   13 11 14 15 44?

POLYBIUS

Back in 1981, kids didn't have home computers or consoles and were forced outside to visit video arcades. In one such arcade in Portland, USA, a video game suddenly appeared. The big, black cabinet only had the word POLYBIUS written on it. The game was addictive and people squabbled to determine who would play next...

Then mysterious Men in Black took the machine away. Some of the players started to suffer from nightmares, headaches and amnesia, and some even vanished, never to be seen again...

Or at least that's the urban legend. There are no photographs of the machine. Was it used to gather data from gamers or was it a recruitment tool used by the government to recruit new agents? We will never know... but Polybius can still be seen cropping up in TV shows (like *The Simpsons*) and comic books.

Steganography means messages can be hidden in lists, such as:

GRAPES

ONIONS

NOODLES

ORANGES

WASABI

Take the first letter of each item – and you have a hidden code: Go now!

STEGANOGRAPHY

The art of hiding messages in plain sight comes from the ancient Greek words: *steganos* (concealed) and *graphein* (writing).

DIGITAL STEGANOGRAPHY

means messages can be hidden within computer files. So a JPEG image of a holiday snap can actually contain text documents of stolen Top Secret files!

Digital techniques can get very sneaky. Imagine looking at a photograph of a little kitten – however, every 10th pixel is a different colour, representing a hidden Morse code message.

KRYPTOS

On the grounds of the CIA's headquarters in Langley, a sculpture by artist Jim Sanborn was erected. Called *Kryptos*, there are four encrypted messages on the sculpture – hidden in plain sight. Three of the codes have been cracked – but the fourth still defies the power of the CIA to break it.

MASTER OF ART

Painter, inventor and artist Leonardo da Vinci was fascinated by codes and hidden messages – many of which have been featured in books and films.

However, in 2010 Luigi Borgia found messages hidden in the eyes of da Vinci's most famous painting: the *Mona Lisa*. One eye contains da Vinci's initials (LV), the other the letters C, E, B, S and 72... or possibly L2.

The meaning of this message has not yet been cracked. What do you think it means?

ULTRAVIOLET INK can be used to write messages across newspaper pages, book covers and even walls. It can only be seen if you shine an ultraviolet light over the writing. Alternatively, invisible ink can be used to hide messages across the page.

behind you

A GOOD AGENT WILL ALWAYS CHECK FOR SIGNS OF INVISIBLE WRITING! ON PAGE 62 YOU WILL DISCOVER THE SECRETS FOR MAKING YOUR OWN UNTRACEABLE INVISIBLE INK!

INVISIBLE INK

Invisible ink has a long history of hiding secrets in the open and it's something that every agent will need to do in a hurry! Here are some techniques to make your own invisible ink while dashing behind enemy lines.

WAX

As a candle melts, it forms long stringy bits of wax. Snap them off and squeeze them together to form a crayon (make sure they've cooled first – no one wants an agent with singed fingers!). Use this wax crayon to write messages that can't be seen.

To read the message, sprinkle talc powder, flour or chalk dust over the page – the dust will stick to the wax and make the message readable.

FRUITY CODES

What you need here is the juice from an apple, orange, or lemon. Grab a cocktail stick and cover the end in juice. Now write the message. If you have no fruit to hand, use milk or vinegar. Give the liquid time to dry!

To reveal the hidden message you need to place the paper in the oven – taking care not to set fire to it! 150°C (or about 300°F) should be just the right temperature. As the paper heats up, the juice will darken and become legible.

If you're worried about setting the kitchen on fire (and the best agents put safety first, after all), try holding it up to a light bulb – not so close that it burns – and the writing will reappear! The only problem is that modern energy-saving bulbs don't produce much heat to make this technique reliable.

BAKING SODA

Add small and equal amounts of baking soda with water (50ml of each should do the trick) into a cup, then mix them together. Using a small paintbrush or cotton bud, use the mixture to carefully write your message and leave it to dry.

To re-read the message you will need some grape juice – the kind out of a carton should do. Dip a brush in the juice and brush the page. The acidic chemical reaction will make the message appear.

A REVEALING CLUE

If your target has written a vital piece of intelligence in a notepad, but then taken the sheet of paper with them, do not despair. They may not have used invisible ink – but you can still make the message reappear.

Carefully take the sheet of paper that was directly underneath the one your target removed. The indent of the pen or pencil they used should have dented the page. You might not be able to see it, but if you use the flat side of a pencil (or a piece of charcoal) to gently rub across the paper, the indentations will remain white and the message will appear!

NUMBERS STATIONS

As you read this, secret codes are buzzing through the air around you – broadcast on shortwave (AM) radio. Known as **NUMBERS STATIONS**, these not-so-hidden codes can be listened to on any radio. They have been on-air ever since WWI, all around the world, broadcasting weird and unusual messages.

Tune into a Numbers Station and you'll probably hear an old nursery rhyme on a loop. Then, at a particular time of day, a voice will suddenly cut in repeating a string of numbers – **SECRET CODES**! The Conet Project has been collecting these mysterious messages and you can listen to some recordings online: https://archive.org/details/ird059

Name:

THE CUBAN FIVE

In 2001, American authorities tried five Cuban intelligence officers in Miami. They received orders from Numbers Stations thought to be run by Cuba's Intelligence agency – the Intelligence Directorate.

Governments run their own Numbers Stations to issue messages to agents anywhere on the planet. It's almost impossible to stop a message, decode it, trace the source or even to pinpoint the location of the agent listening in! This makes Numbers Stations one of the simplest yet most secure, ways of issuing instructions to spies.

The names of some of the more infamous radio stations include the UK's **LINCOLNSHIRE POACHER** and **CHERRY PIE** – the names came from the English folksongs they used to introduce the codes. A Spanish station started their broadcast by shouting 'Atención!', so that became its nickname.

QUANTUM ENCRYPTION

No matter how cleverly a message is encrypted, it has always been possible to break the code – until now! Welcome to the amazing and confusing world of quantum physics.

Now, agencies can send messages and the recipient will know instantly if anybody has looked at the information. How? Well, that's the mind-bending part that involves a university degree and a working knowledge of quantum physics. Here goes!

A single particle of light – known as a photon – can be sent as part of the message. Because of quantum physics, if anybody looks at that photon, it changes into a slightly different photon.

Feel free to read that again, then take a deep breath, and

move on. The recipient will know that the photon has changed – therefore somebody is snooping!

Luckily for spies, computers handle all the complicated code breaking you will need for sending and receiving Top Secret messages.

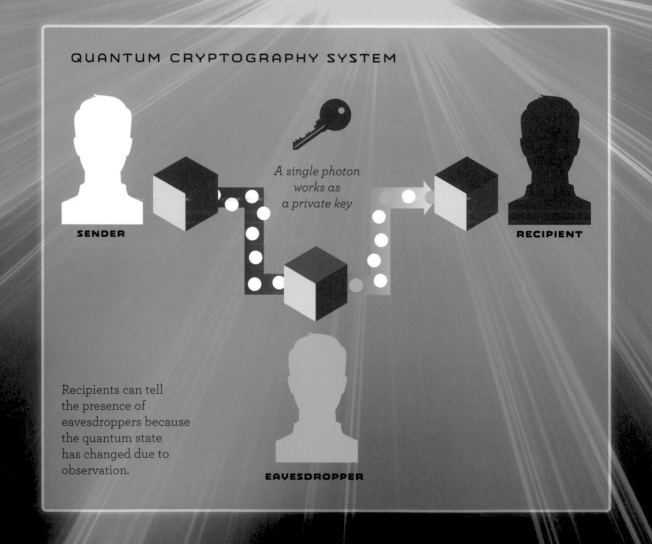

QUANTUM CRYPTOGRAPHY SYSTEM

SENDER

A single photon works as a private key

RECIPIENT

Recipients can tell the presence of eavesdroppers because the quantum state has changed due to observation.

EAVESDROPPER

As you have seen, techniques have come such a long way since Julius Caesar used his substitution code to send messages across the battlefield. As we will discover later, things become even more fiendish when we mix the world of espionage and computers...

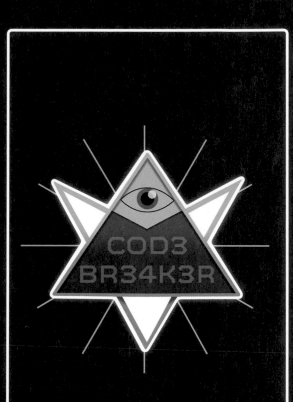

WELL DONE CADET

YOU HAVE NOW
BEEN PROMOTED TO

CODE BREAKER

YOUR SECURITY CLEARANCE HAS BEEN INCREASED, SO NOW YOU ARE READY TO LEARN THE TRICKS OF THE TRADE WHEN WORKING IN THE FIELD!

Leaving the comfortable HQ is your next big step, Agent – get ready to be deployed in the field.

This is the world of **HUMINT** and there is a number of tradecraft skills you must learn.

This is where you'll find out how to spot if your brother really is an **ENEMY AGENT**. Or that your sister has been acting weirdly since the day she was born because she is secretly a **SLEEPER AGENT**! Not to mention your parents – they're always telling you what to do, right? Perhaps they're members of some shady organization!

It's time to find out the truth!

In this section you will be learning essential techniques, such as:

OUT IN THE FIELD

Identifying your **MARK(S)** – this is the person or people you will be following.

Assigning code names, and preparing **COVERT** operations (which take place in secret).

SURVEILLANCE – the art of watching people without their knowledge. You will learn essential surveillance and RECON (short for reconnoitre) methods to observe enemy activity.

Going **UNDERCOVER** by adopting a disguise so good that you can operate in plain sight behind enemy lines.

GO!

A mission could happen at any time – so be prepared with a go-bag. This is a pre-packed bag filled with spy-gear to use at a moment's notice. Keep it near the door or under the bed – somewhere hidden so enemy agents can't find it.

YOUR GO-BAG SHOULD INCLUDE:

 FIELD BINOCULARS – small compact binoculars to be used for surveillance.

 TORCH – a small torch should always be kept handy for night missions or exploring dark locations.

CHALK – to be used to create trail marks and call-out signals (see page 96).

 DISGUISE KIT – wig, cap, glasses, fake nose... (see page 86 for tips).

FAKE ID – have a selection of fake IDs ready for your mission.

PEN & PAD – To jot down any codes you need to crack and make notes of your field observations.

GADGETS – any gadgets you may need for a mission should be ready in your go-bag.

It is important that if you are stopped and searched, enemy agents won't recognize a go-bag for what it is. Hide your tools behind a false lining or the fake bottom of a briefcase.

BOOKS

Books are excellent, and not just for reading! They can also provide a sneaky hiding place for small spy essentials. Take an old book (not this one!) and glue the pages together, except for the first few pages. Next, cut a hollow out in the middle of the book and use it to stash valuable items. To the average person it will look just like a normal book.

GETTING READY FOR FIELD WORK

Before you set foot out of the door, there are some basic skills you need to master.

BLENDING IN

To work successfully in the field, you need to blend into the environment and not draw attention to yourself.

DRESS NORMALLY, choosing sensible, muted colours. If you wear a Hawaiian shirt in the middle of Paris in winter it is likely you will stand out – but wear it with pride if you're in Hawaii and leave the warm coat behind!

DON'T WEAR SUNGLASSES UNLESS IT'S SUNNY! While it might look cool, it will also draw attention. That's exactly why rock stars and actors wear them. If you wear them inside, security people are more likely to stop you for questioning.

ACT CASUAL. Looking worried or frightened creates suspicion. Even if you are lost, walk with confidence. If you are in a restricted area behind enemy lines – such as a school building you are not supposed to be in – act as if you should be there. If you think you belong there then people are less likely to stop you!

STEALTH WALK

No matter how much you blend in, there are times when you have to be stealthier – sneaking through an enemy agent's (sibling's) bedroom is one example. Whatever you do, don't walk on tiptoes, you will lose your balance! Instead, learn to walk like a ninja:

1 EXAMINE THE FLOOR AHEAD. Make sure that there are no obstacles in your way – such as squeaky dog toys, drawing pins, or traps set by the enemy.

2 KEEP YOUR LEGS APART. A shoulder-width should do it. This will spread your weight evenly and ensure you have a firm balance. Keep your knees bent as you take a step to help minimize the noise.

3 KEEP ALL YOUR WEIGHT ON YOUR LEFT LEG. Then take a step with your right leg and slowly push down with the tip of your toes. You want to make sure the floorboard you are stepping on doesn't creak!

4 Now gently push the ball of your foot down so your foot is flat and gradually transfer all your weight onto your right leg. There – you are as **SILENT AS A GHOST**. Now repeat with the left leg.

5 REMEMBER TO BREATHE! Don't hold your breath or you will eventually breathe out in one big gasp! Try not to let your nerves get the better of you – fast, shallow breathing will be louder than your footsteps!

TRACKING

People are messy, which means they are very easy to follow if you know what to look out for. As you will discover, the essential skill for fieldwork is observation.

FOOTPRINTS

Look for footprints. You can tell from the shape if your mark is wearing flat shoes, high-heels or trainers. Depending on how far apart they are you can guess the target's gait – in other words, if they are walking, running or hopping. Somebody walking will have regularly spaced steps, whereas if they suddenly run the steps will be further apart. A runner will hit the ground with their heel first so the heel will dig in deeper.

By matching footprints you can tell if somebody was alone, walking their dog or if they were with another person trading secret information.

SIGNS

Look for broken twigs on the floor, snapped branches at body height that have been pushed aside by your target, or even fragments of cloth that may have been torn on thorns or barbed wire by a spy in a hurry!

Additional signs, such as a trail of flattened grass could indicate that your target was dragging something heavy, like a sack full of stolen documents and other top secret information!

You can also check a target's shoe (assuming they're not wearing it!) for evidence of where they have been. If you suspect your brother may be hiding secrets, you can examine his shoes for signs of **MUD**, **SAND** and even cut **GRASS**, to get an idea of the area he has been walking in. Added together, each little clue could lead you closer to uncovering the truth!

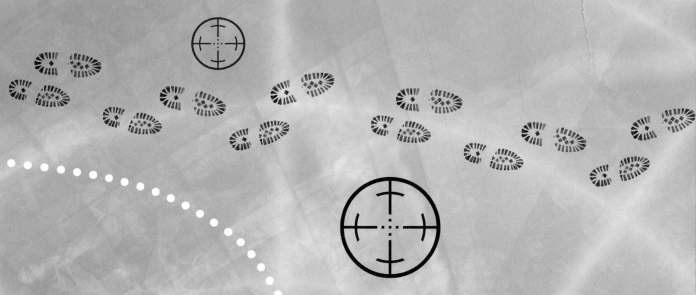

ON THE ROAD

Bicycles, motorbikes, vans and cars can leave very distinctive tyre marks on the ground. A thin tyre indicates a bicycle, slightly wider – a motorbike. Lorries and vans will leave much larger, deeper tracks and may have multiple wheels.

Every brand of tyre has its own tread pattern. The police have a database of different tyre treads so they can quickly identify the make of tyres on the vehicle they are searching for. Why not start making your own list?

Look for patches under a car, or where a car has been parked – if it's dripping water or oil it will give you an idea of the vehicle's condition.

If you do see your suspect jump into a vehicle, make a note of the vehicle type, make, colour and number plate. Different countries have different rules concerning their plates. France has specific numbers indicating the region of country they come from; while Cuba has colour-coded plates depending if the vehicles are taxis, government or privately owned.

Cars across Europe will carry a country code – letters indicating where they are registered. They usually represent the name of the country (F for France, for example), but some are a little trickier, such as CH for... Switzerland.

THE HUMAN TRAIL

Do you realize that you are falling apart even as you read this? Plus, you stink! Don't panic, this is nothing to do with your personal hygiene (let's hope not at least!) – you leave traces of yourself everywhere, and these are microscopic pieces of evidence that can betray you.

FORENSICS

The art of looking for microscopic evidence is called **FORENSIC INVESTIGATION**. Every human body contains **DNA**, the building block of life. And DNA is unique to each person. It's in hair, blood, spit, all of you – and forensic investigators will look for it.

A single strand of hair is enough to identify a person and prove they have been sitting in a car, sleeping in a room or even been bundled into a sack!

On average, people lose 40 to 120 strands of hair every day. In 24 hours you lose an average of 1,000,000 skin cells, which cover your bed or floor, eventually adding to the dust in the room. Every single skin cell or hair identifies you. If you've got a tickle in your nose, don't sneeze! If you do, cover your face – not only is this basic hygiene, but sneezing will leave lots of slimy DNA evidence behind.

Latex gloves can be worn so skin cells from your hands don't contaminate everything you touch, and they will also prevent incriminating fingerprints being left behind. Try to use flesh-coloured gloves instead of the bright blue ones more readily available in shops – they will make you look like a clown!

YOU STINK!

As well as DNA, you have a distinctive scent oozing from your body. You might not be able to smell it and it may be masked by tons of deodorant – but it's there. Dogs can pick up on these smells and use them to track people over long distances.

Police, military and intelligence agencies regularly use canines to track people. It's really tough to mask your odour when behind enemy lines. Crossing through water can kill a **SCENT-TRAIL** dead. However, it won't take long for the dog to pick it up on the other side of the riverbank, so you'll have to move quickly.

SCENT SECRETS

Lots of people think that dogs hate the smell of aniseed, when in fact they love it. So carrying aniseed will probably make the dog more eager to find you! Coffee can help mask your trail from suspicious sniffer dogs – but a trail of coffee will stand out clearly to their human handlers.

FINGERPRINTS

Your fingerprints (and toe prints) are unique to you. Because of the oils in your skin, sweat and the general grubbiness of the room you are in, your fingerprints will end up everywhere if you don't wear gloves.

WHORLS, ARCHES AND LOOPS

The friction ridges on your fingerprints comprise of whorls, arches and loops that twist in unique patterns. Each set of patterns can be matched to discover who it belongs to.

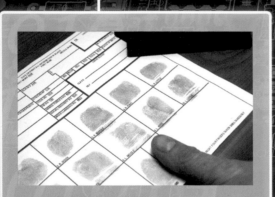

RECORDING PRINTS

Press your suspect's finger on an inkpad then gently place the side of their finger on a sheet of paper and roll it from left to right, leaving a nice black stain on the paper that shows off their fingerprint. Make sure you mark off which finger is which, and from which hand and person they came.

Airports have a more advanced system to scan your fingers without all the messy ink – and this technology is even available on some mobile phones today.

DUSTING FOR PRINTS

Fingerprints are left everywhere, and can be captured from clothing and even feathers. However, the best place to look for them is on smooth surfaces such as windows, tabletops, glasses, cups and door handles. To reveal them, top agents and forensic investigators use a method known as dusting for prints.

A fine powder is sprinkled over the area, and then brushed away. The hope is that any sticky, oily fingerprints will be left behind. These can then be compared to the prints previously taken from suspects until a match is found.

You can find out how to make your own fingerprinting kit on page 126.

FILING PRINTS OFF

Some criminals decide to rub their fingerprints off (a very painful process that should never be tried). They do this in the belief that it will prevent them from being caught. While it is true the skin will grow back, it takes time – and there is nothing that says 'guilty' more than a person with no fingerprints!

SURVEILLANCE

Sometimes you won't know who your target is, or you will have lost all trace of them. Don't give up, this is when the art of surveillance will serve you well.

The most straightforward surveillance technique is the **STAKEOUT**. This is when an agent will stealthily watch a mark's home or HQ for signs of movement. This is often a long and boring task, so essential stakeout gear tends to include drinks and snacks as well as binoculars! Once they make a move, the agent can begin **SHADOWING** them: silently and carefully following them to see where they go.

People are creatures of habit, often taking the same routes to school or the office. If a mark manages to give an agent the slip, the agent will jump ahead and wait (in the nearest coffee shop with a good view of the street, for example) and wait for the mark to pass by.

A-L-E-R-T-!
The best agents will always put safety first. While you're still in training, always make sure you ask your parents for permission before attempting any surveillance, and don't work alone.

If fully fledged agents manage to gain access to their mark's HQ, they'll be sure to look for evidence about the routes the suspect takes. People often throw vital clues in the rubbish bin – so that will be the first port of call. Bins are messy places so latex gloves are needed to keep hands clean. Remember: the thinner the glove the better you'll be able to feel for items hidden inside other objects. It will also stop you leaving **FINGERPRINTS** everywhere.

Particularly good finds are bus or train tickets to regular destinations or receipts for shops the suspect regularly buys coffee or doughnuts from. These will enable the agent to wait at that destination and pick up the mark's trail from there. Agents may also find papers that were *underneath* a sheet on which a secret message was written and can use their spycraft to make that message reappear (as long as they've read Chapter 4 of this book, that is!).

Class Ticket type Adult SGL
STD ANYTIME DAY S ONE
Start Date Number 79872 1571828932
19·SEP Price
From
GLASGOW CEN/QST
To
PRESTWICK A[TRAI]

⊖ London Underground ⊖ London Un[e]
04 JLY 04 D1DAY TRAVELCARD STD
»12«
DAY TRAVELCARD · OFF-PEAK
This side up · Not for re[s]
[Is]sued subject to conditions

VVS
↑
Vor Fahrtantritt entwerten
Please cancel before use
06 10 11:09 Ub
Bitte Rückseite beachten/Please see reverse
3-TageTicket
Stuttgart
für Hotelgäste und
Kongressteilnehmer
Berechtigt nicht zum Vorsteuerabzug
1/ 046671 10,60 €

ıllı 📶 10:44 AM 🔋

Mission briefing

OK, it's time for your first bit of fieldwork. Search your home to find clues to your parents', brother's or sister's activities. Did they take a train? Go to the cinema? Use these clues to build a profile about what they did during their day. You can always ask them directly to see if you were right.

SHADOWING

A mark has been identified, so it's time to start tailing them, with a technique known as **SHADOWING**. This relies on an agent's observational skills and ability to blend in. Here are some top tailing tips used by agents in the field.

Stay three or four metres back and walk casually. Try and follow a mark without looking directly at them – if they suddenly turn around and see someone staring then that is a giveaway and the covert operation is blown!

Walking on the opposite side of the street allows an agent to hide in plain sight, as most people will assume a tail is directly behind them.

If the mark suddenly stops and turns to check for a tail, simply walk on. Pause a little way ahead and casually examine a shop window, using the reflections to watch the target, and wait for them to walk past again.

Stopping to tie a shoelace can also give an agent a good cover while they wait for a mark to catch up.

If the mark has stopped in one place, try to blend in around them. Reading a book – or at least pretending to – allows for stealthy observation of the mark.

Pacing around pretending to have a long phone call is another good technique – but don't make the fake conversation sound too dramatic or the mark may start listening in!

A-L-E-R-T-!
Shadowing can be dangerous, and should only ever be attempted by fully trained, experienced agents. You're just starting out, so if you want to practise, try tailing a friend for a short distance (make sure you ask permission first) and see if you're spotted!

SPOTTING A TAIL

Following marks and enemy agents is one thing, but remember that it works both ways. You might have a **TAIL** of your own! No, you're not turning into an animal – a tail is somebody who is following you. As an agent, it's vital that you know if you are under surveillance yourself.

Change your walking speed – don't start running for no reason, as this will tell enemy agents you have discovered them.

Stop whenever you can to look around, but do it casually. You don't want to draw attention to yourself. Stop to read signposts or kneel and tie your shoelace. Use these moments to recon the area and see if people are looking at you.

While walking, **DOUBLE-BACK** on yourself, checking to see if the same people are following you. Do this in a casual manner – patting your pockets as if you have forgotten something is a good cover.

What's most important is that you never lead a tail to your destination. If you think you're being tailed, it's often better to simply return back to HQ.

Look out for people loitering. They may pretend to be reading – but as you know from the last page, that could be an easy cover because they are looking for you! More advanced spies may use earpieces to talk to Control – so look out for people with headphones who are also keenly scanning the streets.

Security cameras are something a spy should try to avoid although it's never easy. However, the security monitors those cameras are linked to (sometimes visible behind the counter in shops or at the train station) can prove useful when trying to spot a tail.

Stay alert, and keep an eye on the people around you. Does anyone make eye contact with you? Is there someone who stops at the same moment you stop? If so, memorize their faces (see page 84), and look out for them again later.

Corners are the most useful tool you have for avoiding a tail. Turn a corner - then quickly alter your appearance (see page 86) and double-back on your tracks. If done correctly you can walk right past your pursuer without them ever noticing.

If you think you are under surveillance, then it's important to change things up. Stop taking your usual route to your destination – try walking a more scenic route home, or getting off the bus a stop earlier or later than you normally do.

MQTSVXERX: RIZIV EHQMX XLEX CSY LEZI FVSOIR ER IRIQC'W WYVZIMPPERGI SXLIVAMWI XLIC AMPP XVC RIA XVMGOW. MJ CSY ORSA LSA XLIC EVI AEXGLMRK CSY, CSY GER YWI MX XS CSYV EHZERXEKI.

The last top tip has been encoded by HQ. Can you use your newfound code breaking skills to crack it?

RECOGNIZING PEOPLE

If you think you're being followed, you need to be able to memorize people quickly and efficiently and that's all about shapes and colour. Here are some top tips to get faces fixed in your mind:

The first thing to notice is their **HAIR COLOUR** and **STYLE**. Remember though, hair is not a rock solid proof of identity. It can be dyed, cut off, or hidden with a wig or a large hat, so make sure you also take in the **SHAPE OF THEIR HEAD** and the colour of their **SKIN**.

Next look at the windows to their soul – the **EYES**. The shape of the eye is not just linked to where you come from, it's also a genetic trait inherited through your family and is therefore difficult to hide.

MONOLID Flat eyelids that don't have a crease.

HOODED Fold of skin that droops, making the eyelids look smaller.

UPTURNED The lower lid appears larger than the upper lid.

DOWNTURNED Almond shaped eyes that tilt downward.

FACIAL HAIR is another easy identifier - do they have stubble, a beard or moustache? Other items such as **GLASSES** (remember their shape and colour), **SCARS**, **HEARING AIDS**, etc, can be quickly identified. If you have time to commit the mouth shape to memory, do so, and look out for **MISSING TEETH**, **GOLD TEETH** and **BRACES**.

NOSES come in all shapes and sizes too:

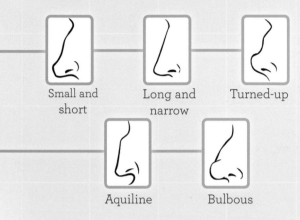

Small and short   Long and narrow   Turned-up

Aquiline   Bulbous

The final things to memorize are **CLOTHING** and **GAIT.** Do they limp, totter along slowly or have long, loping strides? However, since these two aspects can be instantly changed, they are the last thing an agent should focus on.

With practice, an agent will be able to commit a face to memory and notice if they are being followed.

BIOMETRICS

The gathering of all that information is called biometrics and is used by computers for facial recognition. Passports have biometric data stored in their chips. This can also include fingerprint information.

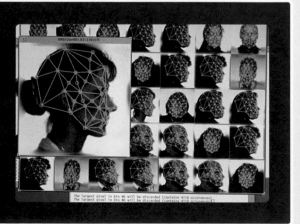

TRANSFORM!

Now you know how to spot if you're being tailed, you need to learn how to use disguises to throw your tail off the scent. A quick disguise on the go can work wonders for a spy.

If you have neat hair, then quickly muss it up. Wearing a **HAT** or a **CAP** will help confuse people, although using a **WIG** will give a better effect! **BALD CAPS** are easily available from most high street gadget shops and are extremely useful for a spy in a hurry!

If you wear **GLASSES**, then not wearing them will confuse a tail (although make sure you wear **CONTACT LENSES** so you are not walking around half-blind!). Likewise, wearing different glasses (with fake lenses so you don't get a headache) will break up the appearance of your face and make you less recognizable.

FAKE MOUSTACHES and **BEARDS** that stick on instantly are a tried and tested method of confounding a tail. Just make sure that they match your hair – there is nothing more eye-catching than somebody with red hair and a black beard. Of course, this is not an ideal option for female agents! Try adding a fake beauty spot and a splash of bright lipstick. It's not as big a transformation as a bushy beard, but it will still cause your pursuers to stop and think.

MAKE-UP can be used to make yourself look older. Try darkening the shadows on your cheeks to make yourself look thinner, or darken under your eyes to make yourself look tired.

Careful not to overdo the make-up as that can also have undesired attention grabbing consequences – a zombie look-alike will draw more attention than a spy!

FALSE NOSES are a great way to confuse people, although make sure it looks real otherwise it will draw the wrong type of attention!

WALK THIS WAY...

Altering the way you walk is an effective disguise. Walking with a slouch indicates low confidence, whereas walking with a straight back and your head held high shows confidence. Practise a range of different walks to help throw your tail off the case, but keep them fairly subtle. A theatrical limp is much more likely to draw attention to you, rather than keep you hidden.

THE WAY YOU SAY IT

If you're good at impressions then try altering your voice. Don't mimic somebody famous – that is sure to attract attention. Instead alter your accent to a different part of the country or even a completely different country. An enemy Agent searching for an American will overlook somebody speaking with a French accent.

Effortlessly speaking with a fake accent will help trick more sophisticated surveillance, such as voice recognition systems.

CLOTHING

If you always wear the same type of clothing then you have established a pattern that an enemy agent can use to easily track you through crowds. On missions, try and vary your outfits and accessories to help you disappear.

Wearing a **BANDAGE** or an **EYE-PATCH** will help change your appearance. Likewise, using liquorice to **BLACK OUT A TOOTH** will give the casual impression that you have a tooth missing. These 'extreme accessories' may well draw attention to you – however, there might be instances when you *want* the enemy to be looking right at you, for instance if you're using decoys (see page 98)!

HATS and **SCARVES** are a quick and easy solution – carrying a selection of different colours and styles means you can change in a hurry. Beware of using loud colours as there is nothing worse that trying to remain inconspicuous wearing a neon-orange baseball cap!

SPY COATS

A favourite trick for professional spies is to wear reversible coats with completely different patterns and colours on the inside. A more advanced jacket can have extendable sections. Inside the pocket is a little cord that, once pulled, drops a weighted inside layer that perfectly matches the outside (and inside) of the coat.

Now a pursuer who was looking for somebody in a short sports jacket will not suspect the agent wearing a long raincoat! The cord can be used to inch the extension back up to the original size.

Shoving a **CUSHION UNDER YOUR COAT** will make you look fatter. The illusion is enhanced (and made more delicious) by placing **MARSHMALLOWS** in your cheeks to make them chubbier. Don't use too many though – a sick spy is not an effective spy!

SPY RINGS

You've almost completed your field operations training, but there are a few more tradecraft skills you need to develop.

Operating alone is difficult for a spy, so it's time to call in some back up and build a spy ring – a team of agents all on the same side. Members of your spy ring can't be just anyone, these should be people who you know you can trust – your best mates, in other words.

Mission briefing

FORM YOUR SPY RING

Begin recruiting friends to form your own spy ring. Make sure all the members of your spy ring know who they are working for and who the **CONTROL** is: you!

Give yourselves **CODE NAMES** – never use each other's real name while out on an operation!

Select targets – other friends and family members who you suspect may be up to no good. Using the surveillance skills you have learned, build up a case file on them.

Include their real names, where they go to school or work – everything you can... but make sure you do it in **SECRET** and write everything down in **CODE**, using the secrets you learned in Chapter 4.

Establish **PASSWORDS** and **COUNTERSIGNS** and even **SECRET HANDSHAKES**. If you are all in disguise then it might be difficult to identify one another and you need to make sure you don't accidentally share your secrets with an enemy!

CREDENTIALS

Sometimes you will need to prove your identity to friendly allies. Almost every intelligence agency has their own ID cards, sometimes called **BADGES** or **CREDENTIALS**.

TASK: MAKE YOUR OWN ID CARD

Be careful not to use your real name or even your code name! Create an alias, a fake name that you will remember and respond to if somebody calls you by it.

Make several different ID cards for specific situations. For example, if you are looking for a friend's lost cat, you could create a CAT FINDING AGENCY card.

C-A-U-T-I-O-N-!
Use your fake ID cards on other enemy agents, not the authorities! They have very hi-tech ways of checking if an identity is real and it could land you behind bars!

COMPANY:

NAME:

AGE:

JOB TITLE:

ACCESS ALL AREAS

RADIO CHATTER

Two-way radios (you might know them as walkie talkies) are essential to keep a team of agents informed during operations. They are more efficient than mobile phones as everybody can talk at once. Use a headset rather than raise the radio to your ear and you'll blend into any environment.

VOICE PROCEDURE

Radio transmission is not secure, so make sure you use code names as often as possible. Some keywords to remember are:

COME IN	'start talking' (for example: 'Bob, come in'.)
AFFIRMATIVE	'yes'.
GO AHEAD	'start talking'.
COPY	'I heard and understood what you said'.
REPEAT	'I didn't understand, say again'.
OVER	'I have finished talking, now reply'.
WILCO	'I will cooperate by carrying out the instructions'.
OUT	'this is the end of the message'.

Code phrases are another shorthand way of communicating. Inventing your own phrases will help confuse enemy agents listening in. For example:

THE WOLF IS IN HIS CRIB	The target is home.
PULL THE PLUG	Abort the operation we have been spotted.

Sometimes the quality of the transmission is not perfect and things can sound fuzzy or crackly. As well as this potential hitch, you need to remember that not everyone pronounces letters the same way. For example: 'zee' if you're American becomes 'zed' if you're British. To avoid confusion, use the phonetic alphabet that is recognized around the world.

A	ALPHA	N	NOVEMBER
B	BRAVO	O	OSCAR
C	CHARLIE	P	PAPA
D	DELTA	Q	QUEBEC
E	ECHO	R	ROMEO
F	FOXTROT	S	SIERRA
G	GOLF	T	TANGO
H	HOTEL	U	UNIFORM
I	INDIA	V	VICTOR
J	JULIET	W	WHISKEY
K	KILO	X	X-RAY
L	LIMA	Y	YANKEE
M	MIKE	Z	ZULU

IF YOU ARE RADIOING A NUMBER PLATE, DON'T SAY 'A56 KLM', SAY 'ALPHA-5-6 KILO LIMA MIKE'.

GETTING CAUGHT

Imagine you're hurrying to meet a fellow agent when the enemy suddenly appears. If they see you together then the whole operation is blown. Shouting a warning will only draw attention to you both. What do you do?

Use personal **GO-SIGNS** to alert your ally. These can be anything you want as long as, before you meet, you make sure you both know the rules of engagement. Both of you will need to regard the other as a complete stranger – no waving or even smiling, that's a dead giveaway!

Go-signs need to be subtle. For example, if one of you is carrying a magazine in your right hand, that's a signal you can 'go' and talk safely. Switching it to the left hand means 'danger', and you are to continue on without a second glance.

If enemy agents intercept you they may **INTERROGATE** you for information. It is important that you reveal nothing of use. The slightest information could be used to attack your agency or even your country! However, you don't have to remain silent. Feeding your enemies **DISINFORMATION** is even better.

Disinformation is intelligence that is incorrect. Sprinkle a few facts in with the disinformation to make it feel more real. For example, if you forgot to do your homework then claiming that 'the dog ate it' probably won't work, but saying 'I forgot it at home because the dog was ill' is more believable because you really did forget!

You will be **SEARCHED**, so it's vital that any intelligence you are carrying is not only encoded, but safely hidden about your person. Check out these secret agent tips and tricks:

FALSE LININGS – sew an extra lining into your jacket (unless it's a reversible one!). Hide the opening so that only you know how to access the secret pocket.

FALSE HEELED SHOE – take an old pair of shoes and detach the heel. Hollow it out and reattach with a single screw so that the heel rotates open and you can hide items inside.

NOW YOU SEE IT...

Specialist spy shops sell some amazing equipment to hide information, such as hollowed-out rings or key fobs and even coins that twist open revealing a space just big enough to conceal a mini SD card.

DIVERSIONS

DECOYS

Now you have a team of secret agents, it will be much easier to throw others off your tail. Decoys are created using props or people to confuse the enemy.

Agents needing to sneak out of bed should never leave it empty – it will be far too noticeable. **STUFF THE BED WITH PILLOWS** so it looks as if there is still a sleeping spy under the duvet, when actually they're long gone!

To enhance the effect, recordings of **SNORING SOUNDS**, can be created using an app or a voice recorder, and left playing next to the pillow. To the casual snoop, it will look and sound as if someone is sound asleep!

For this **SILHOUETTE DECOY** you'll need a large piece of cardboard that you've cut to fit your shape. Place it up against a window and turn on the light in the room so that the cardboard figure is lit from behind. If you have curtains, pull them across so that even the closest examination will not reveal the ploy. Keeping the TV on inside the room will also add to the illusion that somebody is inside.

JACK IN THE BOX

A professional technique for spies in vehicles is to deploy something called a 'jack in the box'. This is an inflatable dummy that looks like the spy and is usually carried in a case.

As the passenger, the spy flees the car as soon as their tail has lost sight of them. The driver quickly inflates the jack in the box on the passenger seat and drives on. Once the tail catches up they will think the passenger is still there.

If you think you are under surveillance, call on a member of your spy ring for help. Go out with a fellow agent **DRESSED EXACTLY THE SAME**! This is your decoy. With luck your enemy will put all their resources in following the wrong person.

Another technique is for your decoy to **DRAW ATTENTION** to themselves – such as falling over, or starting to street-dance. Once everybody is watching them you can slip inside the Top Secret building you were trying to infiltrate!

GOING OFF THE GRID

With the rise of technology, it's almost impossible to avoid detection (known as going 'off the grid'). Everywhere you go you leave a trail that can be used to find you – even if you don't want to be found.

Let's look at an example. You are going to take a ride from one side of the country to the other. That should be simple enough, right? Just be warned that you are leaving a trail known as a 'digital footprint' everywhere...

You jump into a **CAR** – which is registered with the relevant government driving agency. So is the name and address of the driver.

If you stop for **FUEL OR FOOD**, the local service station will have its own surveillance cameras that register **VEHICLE NUMBER PLATES** and monitor public areas for safety.

If you pay for food on a **BANK CARD** then the transaction is immediately registered with the time, amount spent and the exact location where you made the purchase. If you use a shop loyalty card they will also keep a record of everything you have purchased. So every tin of beans bought using a loyalty card is registered on a computer somewhere!

Along the roads there are numerous **SURVEILLANCE CAMERAS** keeping an eye out for crime. Close Circuit TV (CCTV) monitors traffic flow to avoid traffic jams and accidents, and speed cameras photograph the number plate and driver if they are going too fast.

As you can see, your every move is observed. It's just as bad if you get on a **BUS OR TRAIN**. Once the ticket is purchased there is a record of which card was used to make the purchase, who the card is registered to and where you are heading. On top of that, most buses and trains have their own CCTV.

SLAB CITY

Despite the difficulty in keeping off the grid, there are societies around the world who do it successfully. Slab City in California, USA boasts that it is the last free place in America. Located near the Mexican border are hundreds of people living amongst the ruins of an old World War II base, housed in mobile homes.

There is no water, electricity, gas, sewer systems or even shops, so the entire community is self-sufficient and lives off the land. For a spy needing to keep his head low, it can be a useful place to hide...

So, you try going on **FOOT** instead. If you know where all the CCTV cameras are located you can weave between them to avoid detection – but then you use your phone to call a friend. Bad move. Remember triangulation? If you forgot to turn off the GPS on the phone then they will instantly be able to pinpoint your position down to the very centimetre of ground you're standing on.

If you use your **COMPUTER** to access, well anything, your IP address is logged and can be used to locate and identify the exact computer you are on (you'll learn more about this in Chapter 8).

The only true way to go off the grid is to use no technology at all and **CAMP** rather than live in a normal house.

CONGRATULATIONS

CODE BREAKER

YOU ARE NOW TRAINED
IN FIELD ESPIONAGE AND
HAVE OFFICIALLY BEEN
PROMOTED TO

JUNIOR AGENT!

-.-- --- ..- .- -. / .... . -.. .- .- -. .. - .-- / .-.. . ... .- . -. / .... , -.-- / -... .-.. / .. . .-. . -. / .... . -.. .-.-. / -- -. --- --- -.. / .-. . .- .- -. / .. . -. . / - .... . / .-. .. . .-.- -. -.-.

You're midway through your training and already shaping up to be a very useful spy. However, right now even a pigeon could do your job! If you don't believe it, then take a break from your training and step into the amazing world of animal spies...

ANIMAL SPIES

Animals have long been trained as spies because they are able to go places people can't reach and they generally don't arouse suspicion.

The first battlefield drones were **PIGEONS** during World World I. The German army attached cameras to them to photograph Allied trenches. By World War II, the Allies experimented with using homing pigeons housed in the nose cones of rockets. They steered the engines by pecking on controls. Yes, seriously!

Pigeon spies were essential during D-Day. Instead of using radios that could be intercepted, pigeons carried messages giving enemy positions. They were so valuable that 32 pigeons were awarded the UK's highest award for animal valour: **THE DICKIN MEDAL**. Eighteen dogs, three horses and a cat were also honoured during World War II.

During the Cold War **RAVENS** and **RATS** were trained to drop – and later retrieve – remote bugging equipment. Who would suspect a raven of planting a microphone on the windowsill where a Top Secret meeting was taking place?

WARRIOR BEAR

During World War II, the Second Polish Transport Company found a young bear wandering the hills. The unit fed him and named him **VOYTEK**. As he grew he was trained to carry guns and ammunition and he even learned to salute.

IQ ZOO

Leading animal trainers Marian Breland Bailey and Keller Breland opened the IQ Zoo in Arkansas, USA. It was a popular tourist destination where people could see trained chickens walking tightropes, rabbits riding mini fire engines and raccoons playing basketball. What the public didn't know was that in a special area of the zoo, animals were being trained as spies!

The duo were responsible for several advancements in the world of animal spies. They helped mastermind the **ACOUSTIC KITTY** (see below), they trained ravens to carry bugging equipment and even pioneered a technique to make birds alert soldiers to possible ambushes. Even today, their work is still classified Top Secret.

PROJECT ACOUSTIC KITTY

This has to be one of the best secret project names invented by the CIA. In the 1960s, batteries and microphones were implanted in cats, with the antenna in their tails. The cats would prowl around, picking up and transmitting conversations.

A cat's first mission was to eavesdrop on two men outside the Soviet Embassy in Washington DC. But, a few minutes after it began its task, the feline ran under a taxi and was sadly killed.

The project was finally abandoned when they realized that the cats would rather run after food than spy for humans.

DEEP WATER

Hidden in the oceans are some of the cleverest animal spies on the planet – **DOLPHINS**. For over 40 years, dolphins have been successfully spying for the US Navy, and they take their wages in fish!

After training, dolphins can detect mines that could sink a warship and they can even mark them for deactivation by their human handlers. The Kitsap-Bangor naval Base in Washington is patrolled by a pod of trained dolphins on the lookout for swimmers or divers in the restricted waters.

When an enemy is found, the dolphins touch a special sensor on the side of a boat to alert their handler. The handler then attaches a light or tracking device to the dolphin's nose, which the dolphin will attach to the intruder so the humans can find him.

SEA LIONS are also deployed in naval bases and are used in protecting the US fleet in the Persian Gulf. These seals carry a special clamp in their mouths that they attach to an intruder's leg. The sea lions move so fast that the intruder only becomes aware of it when the rope – attached to the clamp – rapidly reels them aboard a ship where security personnel are waiting.

THE UNUSUAL SUSPECTS

Some animals might receive spy training, but there are many that do not, and still get accused of espionage! Check out these badly blamed beasts:

6'6"

6'0"

5'6"

5'0"

4'6"

4'0"

3'6"

3'0"

Panic erupted in 2007 when the Iranian army captured **SQUIRRELS** lurking around a nuclear enrichment plant.

A year later, two **PIGEONS** were also arrested for spying.

In Saudi Arabia, officials arrested a **VULTURE** in 2011 because they thought it was working for the Mossad.

In 2013, Egyptian authorities arrested a **STORK** for espionage after mistaking the plastic migration tag fastened to its leg for a miniature spying device.

Perhaps the weirdest suspected spy was the **MONKEY** allegedly hanged in Hartlepool, UK, during the Napoleonic war. And the charge? The monkey was accused of being a Frenchman.

LITTLE SPIES

The world of animal espionage is very creative and increasingly unusual.

BOMB-SNIFFING BEES

Take a look, for example, at bomb-sniffing bees. Honeybees have a superb sense of smell thanks to their sensitive antennae. They are intelligent insects and can be trained to pick up the scent of bomb-making ingredients.

The goal is to have a box from which a group of bees could sniff the passing air. If they detect any bomb-like substances, they all wave their proboscises (the bee equivalent of a nose) at the same time – a movement that is recognized by a computer, which triggers an alarm.

TERROR GERBILS!

When you are frightened, your heart beats faster, your pulse quickens and a drug called adrenalin is released into your body. It's a natural reaction that you can't stop... and it turns out that gerbils are particularly good at sniffing out adrenalin.

The Mossad pioneered the sniffing-gerbil technique in the 1970s. Furry agents were stationed in Tel Aviv airport to sniff out terrorists who were pumped up with adrenalin because of the terrible acts they planned to commit.

MI5 experimented with the system but soon discovered a flaw. People afraid of flying also had increased adrenalin levels and the gerbils were identifying innocent people as potential terrorists.

ROBO-SPY

Technology improves spying techniques – and in the case of animals, it turns them into **SUPER-SPIES**.

The US Department of Defense has created a method of implanting electronics into insects during their larval stage. These devices allow scientists to control the insects – literally by remote control. **COCKROACHES** have been created that can be guided around enemy buildings to steal data or record sensitive conversations. Other insects have been given sensors to detect chemical attacks – all controlled by a human operator.

It won't be long before a spy's go-bag includes a little matchbox containing a robo-cockroach that can be used to, literally, bug a room!

Insects are small and versatile, but to carry heavier equipment, such as cameras, you need a bigger mount. Let's call in the **RATS**! Rats are already incredibly smart and can be trained like pigeons and ravens. Scientists have created a chip that fits into a rat's brain and enables an operator to guide the rat through an obstacle course using a series of electric impulses.

Imagine controlling a robo-rat, carrying a spy camera, through the narrowest of cracks in a building, sneaking into buildings via the sewer system or even crawling through rubble and debris to perform search and rescue missions. How cool would that be?

One of the most exciting things about being promoted to Junior Agent is that it's now time for your gadget training. Spies have always needed ways of carrying information and special devices to help avoid being spotted or caught – otherwise they wouldn't be very good spies.

In the movies, James Bond became famous for his use of hi-tech devices – from laser watches to gyrocopters that could fit in a suitcase – supplied by Q-Branch, a fictional division of MI6. In the movies the Quartermaster – known as Q – would provide him with exactly the right gadget for the mission ahead. In reality, a spy will have no idea what to expect, so needs to be armed with a range of gadgets.

DIRECTORATE OF TRAINING AND DEVELOPMENT was MI6's secret lab that created gadgets during the World War II. Their inventions included

a red-light torch (ideal for snooping in the dark without drawing attention to a bright white light); gun silencers so the enemy would never hear the bang; and knockout drugs to put guards to sleep.

Today, the majority of amazing gadgets come out of America's **DARPA (DEFENSE ADVANCED RESEARCH PROJECTS AGENCY)** created in 1958 in response to Russia launching the world's first satellite, Sputnik. Now DARPA's mission is to come up with surprising advanced technology. Here are some of their biggest hits:

JETPACKS AND EXO-SKELETONS

Some gadgets might sound completely futuristic – like jetpacks – but they have actually been around since 1959, and have been most widely used by astronauts to help them work outside their spacecraft. But on Earth they are not yet in use, mostly due to their limited range. Nobody wants a spy who drops out of the sky!

Powered exo-skeletons offer the chance to build super-Agents in the future. Imagine being able to lift an entire car, run much faster or jump further than before - that's the future of bionic Agents!

But why wait for the future? The US military is already developing HULC – Human Universal Load Carrier – allowing soldiers to carry up to 90kg (200lb) and move at 16km/h (10 mph).

BIGDOG

Carrying heavy equipment slows the progress of agents and soldiers. While horses are one solution, they need to be cared for and fed. Wouldn't it be great to have a robotic steed to do that for you? Enter the amazing BigDog.

Designed and built for DARPA by Boston Dynamics, BigDog is able to trot along carrying 110kg (243lbs) – whether it is equipment or injured soldiers being carried off the battlefield. Everything is controlled by an onboard computer that determines BigDog's route. If it stumbles or falls, it can pick itself up, so there is no need for a human operator to control it.

WILD CAT is their next step, able to gallop along at 25km/h (16mph) – which is probably faster than you can run!

I SEE YOU!

Seeing in the dark was once thought to be an ability only available to cats, but as a secret agent you need to be just as alert in the dead of night as in the daytime. Welcome to the world of night vision...

THERE ARE TWO TYPES OF NIGHT VISION.

SPECTRAL RANGE

(better known as **THERMAL IMAGING**) uses infrared to detect heat emitted by objects and can be used in absolute darkness. Blue represents cooler colours and red the warmest. This makes it very tricky to hide, as thermal imaging technology allows you to see people behind curtains and walls. Spies can wear special clothing that absorbs body heat. It might make you sweat, but you will blend into the background and its cooler blue shades.

INTENSITY RANGE

amplifies the *tiniest* amounts of illumination that your eyes are normally unable to see. These images appear in greys or greens, so it's impossible to distinguish colours. This is the most common night vision used, as it has a better range, but the disadvantage is that it requires *some* light to work, even weak moonlight. It is also easy to defeat – if somebody shines a light directly into your goggles then you'll be temporarily blinded!

STOP BUGGING ME!

Watching an agent from a distance is one thing, but unless you are a skilled lip-reader, you won't know what they are saying. This is why **AUDIO SURVEILLANCE** is an essential tool for you.

Listening devices, known as **BUGS**, can be planted in a room before an enemy's important meeting. You can hide them in anything – from curtains, pictures and phones to light bulbs, ornaments and even on pets! Of course, you can also obtain a bug-detecting gadget to **SWEEP** a room for hidden microphones.

Bugs transmit using **SHORTWAVE FREQUENCIES** – meaning that the receiver needs to be close by, so check for any suspicious-looking delivery vans outside!

Your mobile phone can be tricked-out with devices such as bug detectors and even radiation monitors, making it easier for you to track any stolen nuclear missiles, all from your phone!

FEEL THE VIBES!

Physics may not be every student's favourite subject, but it is very important to the eavesdropper! When you talk, your voice bounces off everything in the room – including the windows. This causes the glass to vibrate, just like a speaker. Shining a laser on the window can pick up those vibrations. Once linked to a computer – hey presto – you have bugged the room!

KEEPING CONTROL

Sometimes force needs to be used in the field – but not so much that people actually get hurt! Maybe you are trained in martial arts, such as kung fu or karate, which enables you to defend yourself when you have to. But if you're not, and you find yourself in a sticky situation in the field, there are some very cool tools available.

SPRAY IT

Sprays come in all shapes and sizes. The larger ones are used for controlling a riot (but an agent may find themselves on the receiving end of one!).

You probably use a deodorant when you are sweaty, but **MALODORANTS** are the complete opposite. The Israeli army use **SKUNK** to scatter crowds. This chemical water smells like sewage and is very difficult to wash off. Smelling that bad makes it easier to tail an agent on the run!

PEPPER SPRAY is a liquid that uses a chemical taken from plants that irritates the eyes and skin and makes breathing difficult. The target will be in so much pain they won't be much of a threat. A nastier version of this is **TEAR GAS,** which can be used to control mobs.

STICKY FOAM

Imagine trying to run away from an enemy, covered in a foam that is slowly expanding to hamper your movements – and that then solidifies, trapping you like a fly in amber! That's exactly what sticky foam does. It can also glue your feet to the floor!

GUNS

We all know guns are **BAD NEWS**, and a good agent shouldn't need one. Spying is about stealth! However, it can sometimes be necessary to have a little backup in your belt, such as a **NET GUN** that tangles your victim up in a thick net. The nets can be made from fabric or lightweight metals, so not even the strongest person can break free!

Tranquillizer guns fire darts that send your targets to sleep. These darts sting a little, but they are safe enough to use on both people and animals.

SIGHT AND SOUNDS

Ever had somebody take a surprise photo of you and the camera's flash has left white spots in front of your eyes? Now imagine the **LED INCAPACITATOR**. It fires different coloured pulses of light straight into your eyes that gives you a splitting headache, making you throw up... and then temporarily blinding you.

If you've been clever enough to wear sunglasses then you still need to beware of **SONIC WEAPONS**. These tools can stun or confuse victims – and even make them desperate to run to the toilet – using a special range of sound frequencies.

As you grow older, everybody gradually loses a little hearing, which means some sounds can only be heard by children and teenagers but no longer by adults. A device called **THE MOSQUITO** plays loud and annoying audio signals at 14,000 Hz – perfect to put teenagers off hanging around street corners, but inaudible to adults' ears...

COOL CARS

At this stage in your training, it is unlikely that you will find yourself behind the wheel of the latest sports car or piloting a supersonic aircraft. However, it's important that you are aware of the range of awesome vehicles being used around you and what they can do. And you never know, one day they might just be yours...

While movie spies always seem to have the coolest cars, a real agent needs to blend in – not stand out! There is nothing more attention-grabbing than arriving in a sleek Aston Martin with missiles shooting from the boot! But in reality, a useful spy car will look exactly like the other rusting vehicles on the road.

However, that's not to say that an innocent-looking car won't have some neat tricks up its sleeve.

If you're shadowing a red car but lose it as it turns a corner, you are not likely to suspect the black car parked to one side... which is exactly why **HEAT PAINT** is perfect. Warm the car's bodywork and it instantly changes colour – utterly confusing your tail!

WHO NEEDS A DRIVER?

You won't be able to drive just yet, but that doesn't mean a Junior Agent can't have their own car. Google is pioneering driverless cars (known as **AUTONOMOUS VEHICLES**), so one day you can travel to school without all the hassle of having to talk to your parents. Driverless cars will allow agents to perform more important tasks while travelling. The US military have trucks to carry supplies across dangerous enemy terrain. They use a combination of GPS tracking and radar linked to an onboard computer that makes all the decisions.

ROBO-TANK

Robo-trucks are one thing, but allowing robots to make life-or-death decisions sounds like something from a science fiction film, right? Wrong! It's happening right now in Russia! Dubbed the **MOBILE ROBOTIC COMPLEX**, these war-robots have been created to guard missile sites in Russia and can make decisions without ever having to consult a human. Now you know about them, you won't waste precious time trying to talk to a driver who isn't there!

DIGITAL NUMBER PLATES can be made to look like the real thing but are controlled by computer so they can change instantly.

3X 5N

SPY BOATS

No terrain should be out of bounds for a determined agent – and that includes the oceans. Hiding in the depths is an easy way to avoid detection and submarines are the natural stealth vehicles of the sea.

Of course, if you're travelling the seven seas on the surface, there

THE SEA SHADOW

From the minds of DARPA comes this experimental boat built by the American company Lockheed Martin. State-of-the-art stealth technology and the special angular-shaped hull makes it invisible to radar, allowing it to slip unnoticed through the water. This radical ship design has been used in more recent stealth boats, like the US Navy SEALs' high-speed Sealion project, designed to get agents and troops in and out of enemy territory.

And then there is the **M80 STILETTO** whose hull design means it can go very fast in shallow water (about 93km/h, 58mph), and is extremely stealthy.

When you are near the sea, be on the lookout for any of these strange boats. You never know what Top Secret activities are taking place right under your nose!

THE ART OF STEALTH

In your field training you learned how to walk quietly to avoid detection – this is the art of **STEALTH**. When it comes to moving a huge boat or even an aeroplane around then it's a little more difficult. Look at them – they're big and cool-looking – surely anybody would notice them?

These vehicles are usually detected on **RADAR** long before anybody sees them, allowing enemies to shoot at them from afar. But what if you could make materials and create a shape that doesn't reflect radar waves? In that case the vehicle would be **INVISIBLE** to radar... and that's the trick to a stealth vehicle.

SPY PLANES

These aircraft fly near the very top of the list of cool spy gadgets. They are painted in dark blue – almost black – so that they are nearly invisible at night. But they include other special features designed to make them ideal spy planes.

U-2
MACH 0.6 OR 730 KM/H (460 MPH)
RANGE: 10,300 KM (6,400 MILES)

U-2

Built by Lockheed in 1955 during the Cold War, America's U-2 was Top Secret until Francis Gary Powers was shot down over the Soviet Union in 1960. It flew slowly, enabling the state-of-the-art surveillance cameras to take very detailed pictures and gathering SIGINT from 21,330m (70,000ft) – twice the height a passenger plane flies.

The U-2 was the undoubted king of the skies and it is such a great aircraft that it's still in use today!

In case a U-2 crashed in enemy territory, the CIA came up with a cover story claiming that it was used solely for high-altitude weather research. Oddly enough, they use a similar cover story every time the public report a UFO...

Before technology shrunk the size of cameras, the U-2 carried these massive film cameras in its payload bay.

21,330 M
(70,000 FT)

SR-71 BLACKBIRD
MACH 3.3 OR 4,040 KM/H (2,500 MPH)
RANGE: 5,150 KM (3,200 MILES)

SR-71 BLACKBIRD

In the early 1960s, Lockheed struck again with their SR-71 Blackbird and created a design that many still consider one of the most stunning in aviation. Although it could not fly as far as the U-2 without refuelling, it was much faster – able to reach anywhere in the world within hours.

Travelling at over three times the speed of sound, if an enemy shot at the Blackbird, it would simply speed up and out-race the missile!

It moved so quickly that the titanium body would expand with the heat. To stop it bursting apart, the designers left gaps in the aircraft's panels. On the runway it would leak fuel, but once it took off the body expanded to perfectly seal the gaps.

**ORDINARY
PASSENGER PLANE**
MACH 0.92 OR 1,130 KM/H (700 MPH)
RANGE: 14,800 KM (9,200 MILES)

**24,390 M
(80,000 FT)**

**10,700 M
(35,000 FT)**

DRONES

UAVs (Unmanned Aerial Vehicles) are more commonly known as drones. These small lightweight aircraft have no pilots onboard and work like radio-controlled model aircraft – except flying far greater distances and armed with anything from missiles to high-definition surveillance cameras.

The drone pilots are thousands of miles away – often in completely different countries – flying the UAVs from the safety of a command centre near their homes.

The great thing about drones is that you can buy your very own small ones, equipped with cameras, so you can do your own aerial snooping! You'll need to save up some pretty serious pocket money though. By practising on the smaller ones today, who knows what you will be piloting in the future?

DRONING ON...

As a spy, you should always keep one eye on the sky to see if anybody is spying on you. Here's a handy spotter's guide to drones:

– the **IAI EITAN** is an Israeli UAV primarily designed for SIGINT gathering. It is able to stay in the air for about 70 hours and travel at 370km/h (230mph).

– the **MQ-9 REAPER** is an American drone designed for combat. Flying for up to 14 hours at 312km/h (194 mph), the remote pilots are able to launch deadly missiles at a target.

– **TARANIS** is the next generation of UAV, built in the UK. Like the Reaper, it is armed to the teeth – but it also has the advantages of having stealth capabilities.

STEALTH AIRCRAFT

In your current duties, there will be no call for you to be flying in a stealth aircraft, but you still need to know about them. Who knows if an enemy agent is secretly planning to use one to flee the country?

While the U-2 and Blackbird relied on flying high and fast, they could still be detected on enemy radar. The latest generation of spy planes use **STEALTH TECHNOLOGY** to avoid being detected on radar, allowing them to fly slower and lower without being seen. In addition, these aircraft don't just carry cameras – they can be armed with **WEAPONS.**

F-117 NIGHTHAWK

Lockheed's secret development HQ is nicknamed the **SKUNK WORKS** and their crowning triumph is the **F-117 NIGHTHAWK**. Originally code-named **HAVE BLUE**, it is commonly called the stealth fighter. The odd design was considered groundbreaking but the pilots thought it was ugly and gave it the nickname of the **GOBLIN**. It was a true ghost of the skies – invisible to radar so the enemy wouldn't even know you have flown overhead. It stopped service in 2008 and was replaced by the F-22 Raptor.

B-2

Like something out of a Batman movie comes Northrop Grumman's **B-2 SPIRIT**, which is primarily a stealth bomber capable of firing missiles. On radar the enemy would only see something the size of a pigeon approaching before it was too late...

SATELLITES

Travelling to school, you may think that spy satellites have no effect on you at all. Think again! Global Positioning Satellites (GPS), created by the US Military, allow you to navigate anywhere in the world. Even as a Junior Agent you will have access to these amazing gadgets!

From the moment the Soviet Union started the space race in 1957 with the launch of the very first satellite (**SPUTNIK**), it was clear that space was going to revolutionize spying. All Sputnik could do was broadcast a signal, whereas modern **SPY SATELLITES** (officially called **RECONNAISSANCE SATELLITES**) are capable of so much more. They are now used to gather **IMINT**, **SIGINT** and **MASINT**.

Early satellites were able to take photographs of enemy bases from orbits as high as 200-400 miles above the Earth – much higher than is possible for any aircraft. The film was then parachuted back down to Earth so that it could be studied.

Now, satellites are able to beam the images direct to spy HQs on the ground. Furthermore, rather than just high-resolution photographs, they are able to send video and audio too. These satellites are commonly referred to as **KEYHOLE SATELLITES** because, like looking through a keyhole in a door, you can see a small section of the ground below.

For your own spying missions, you can access images like those from satellites. There are online maps, such as Google Maps, Bing Maps and Apple maps that show images of your local area as if they were taken from an orbiting satellite. You can even zoom in on your own house!

Map data ©2015 Google

SATELLITE KILLERS

If you know there is a satellite spying directly overhead, what can you do about it? It's time to deploy your **ANTI-SATELLITE WEAPONS (ASAT)**. There is a variety of missiles that can be fired from the ground to destroy enemy satellites, and they have even been used to bring down satellites threatening to plummet to Earth.

But there are more devious satellites out there – such as Russia's Kosmos 2499 which is suspected to be a **SATELLITE KILLER**. Able to change orbit, these satellites can move in close to another enemy satellite and destroy it.

But what about satellites that spy on *other* satellites? They exist too. Called **SATELLITE INSPECTORS**, they fly close to an enemy satellite to listen in on communications. False information can also be fed into them to confuse an enemy!

MAKE YOUR OWN GADGETS

You're almost ready to become a fully fledged Field Agent... but before you do, your spy agency needs its very own gadget armoury. You're going to need gadgets to survive out there!

The good news is that fantastic gadgets are more easily available than you might think. With a little investigation and a lot of saving, you can purchase bugging equipment, nightvision gear, remote surveillance cameras and even your own drones!

MAKE YOUR OWN
NIGHT-VISION LIGHT

For sneaking around in the dark you will need a torch. However, nothing will draw attention to you more than a bright white light! The white light will also destroy your natural night vision, meaning when the light is turned off you will be able to see nothing at all! To prevent this, you need a night-vision light!

You will need:
A torch
Red cellophane
Sticky tape

- Cut a circle of transparent red cellophane – the kind sweets or some foods are wrapped in is perfect – and tape it over the lens of your torch - you now have a light perfect for snooping in secret.

- The red light will also preserve your night vision so that when you turn it off, you will still be able to see something if there's a still a little light available.

PERISCOPE

When conducting surveillance, there's nothing better than being able to see around corners or over countertops – which makes periscopes perfect!

For decades submarines have been able to remain hidden beneath the waves thanks to the use of mirrors mounted in the periscope at 45° angles, which bounces light perfectly into the viewer's eye. The good news is they're very easy to make.

You will need:
The template below
Two small mirrors
(ideally from a make-up kit)
Glue and scissors

- Copy the template below – extending the body to any length you require – onto a sturdy piece of cardboard.

- Cut and fold the cardboard tube as indicated. Make sure the sections labelled 'mirror' are folded over (see the diagram above). If your lines are straight, they will rest at a perfect 45°.

- Ensure the periscope is firmly glued together and you have a perfect periscope!

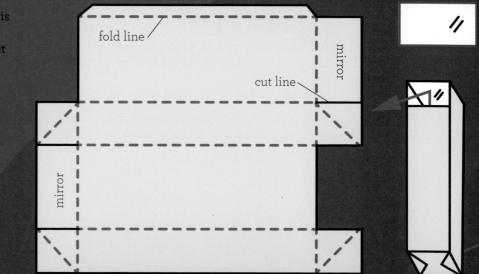

FINGERPRINTING KIT

Keeping a record of your friends and foes is essential – and one of the most accurate ways to do this is by building a library of fingerprints. A good agent will always have a fingerprint kit to hand.

You will need:

- A container to keep everything together
- A pencil and sharpener
- Small jar to keep powder in
- A small soft paint or shaving brush
- Clear sticky tape
- An album to store fingerprints
- Ink pad
- Paper

1 Keeping everything together in the same box will help you be ready at all times. To take a fingerprint (remember your training, look on smooth surfaces) you will first need to make it visible. Here is how you will use your kit:

2 Sharpen a pencil and crush the graphite shavings that come off it into a fine powder. Just put the tip of the pencil into the sharpener to avoid getting lots of wood shavings mixed up in your graphite.

3 Sprinkle the graphite powder over the suspected fingerprint then carefully dust it off using the soft brush. If there is a fingerprint it will become visible!

4 Next, cut a length of sticky tape and gently place it over the revealed fingerprint. Softly dab the tape down using the brush... then carefully peel back – and the fingerprint will be transferred to the sticky tape!

5 To care for the print, place it in a book where you can go back and compare it. Remember to make a note of the time and place you took the print. If you're very hi-tech, you can even scan it into your computer. Now you need to compare the prints to your suspects.

Ideally you can ask your target for their fingerprints and take them using the inkpad and paper. Once you have them, you can compare the whorls, arches and loops (as we learned in chapter 5) to see if they match.

Alternatively you can sneakily take fingerprints from objects your target has recently handled. If they are drinking from a cup or a glass, try and get hold of it before it's washed, and the evidence is destroyed.

MAKE YOUR OWN
MIRRORED SHADES

You have learned a number of techniques to spot a tail but here is a gadget you can make yourself to help you spot if an enemy is behind you.

You will need:
A pair of large sunglasses
An old CD
Glue and scissors

Caution: if the sunglasses are too small, all you will see are your ears!

• Carefully cut the CD so the shape matches a small portion of the sunglasses' outer edge as indicated.

• Once you have the right shape, glue them into place onto the inside of the sunglasses' lens.

• With these sunglasses, you will look cool and be able to spot a tail!

FIELD AGENT

YOUR TRAINING IS ALMOST OVER – YOU'RE NO LONGER A

JUNIOR AGENT

YOUR SECURITY CLEARANCE HAS BEEN RAISED TO

FIELD AGENT!

This is it, Field Agent – your final training session, and one that takes your spycraft skills online. In this section, you will learn cybersecurity – the art of protecting yourself online from the ever-vigilant cyber snoops.

THE INTERNET

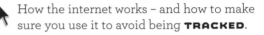

Modern espionage is moving off the field and onto the internet and in this chapter you will learn such vital skills as:

➤ How the internet works – and how to make sure you use it to avoid being **TRACKED**.

🖑 The art of online **ENCRYPTION** and security.

⧗ The secret uses of **VIRUSES**, malware and the hidden nasties of the internet.

Approximately two billion people around the world use the internet every day, which explains why it can sometimes be slow!

It started life in 1969 as **ARPANET**, a US military system for sending messages between computers using **PACKET SWITCHING**.

Packets of information are sent through several computer **ROUTERS** around the world. Like a postman, each router forwards the packet on to the correct address (a **URL** or **EMAIL** address).

Packets can run in any direction around the world, passing through computer **SERVERS** and travelling through fibre optic cables under the oceans or bouncing off satellites until they reach the address. If you drew the route of an invidividual packet, it would look like a series of crisscrossing lines – which is why we call it the **NET** or **WEB**.

THE FATHER OF THE WEB

With the basic structure of the internet in place, what was needed was a method to allow anybody to send messages and create pages for people to browse. In 1989, British scientist Tim Berners-Lee created the rules and software that we all use today: the HyperText Transfer Protocol (that's the HTTP at the start of every URL), the code to make webpages – HTML (HyperText Markup Language), and a web browser to use it all. He gave this all to the world for **FREE**.

PACKET SWITCHING

This is what powers the internet. If you want to send a friend a piece of information, such as a picture, your computer splits it into chunks called packets. Each packet is sent to the recipient – just like cutting a letter up into hundreds of parts and getting different postmen to deliver them.

The recipient's computer collects the packets and sends an acknowledgement that it has been received. If your computer doesn't get an acknowledgement it will send it again. Imagine some of the postmen have been chased by dogs or fallen into a shark tank – you send the missing packets out with different postmen who take *different routes* to the recipient.

Long before the World Wide Web, the Arpanet system and others were used by governments and spies to send secrets. Now the internet is an essential tool for all intelligence organizations.

KEYWORDS

URL: Uniform Resource Locator, the internet equivalent of an address.

IP ADDRESS: A string of numbers that identify printers, webcams, routers, and computers. It contains information about *what* it is and *where* it is located.

HYPERTEXT: The text displayed on a computer.

HTML: HyperText Markup Language is the standard computer code used to create internet pages.

SERVER: A computer that stores internet pages, emails and passes messages along – a combination of a post office sorting room and a library.

MIND-BENDING ENCRYPTION

With all this information zipping around the internet, anybody can look at it. So you need a way to make it secure. Your training has taught you some code basics, but now you will have to get to grips with brain-boggling computer-encryption.

The 'simplest' way for you to encrypt a message is to us a SECRET-KEY. You 'lock' your message with a key and send it on its way. The person you want to read the message has an identical key that unlocks the message. So far, so good. But this key isn't like the key to get into your house, it's a bunch of numbers. This might make things seem really complicated, but in fact you have already been doing this with some of the codes you learned earlier in your training.

Think about the 26 letters of the alphabet. A simple substitution cipher would replace a letter with a number. Knowing that 1=A is the secret key that unlocks this message:

23, 5, 12, 12

4, 15, 14, 5,

1, 7, 5, 14, 20!

Cracked it? Great work! Now, onto something a little more complex. Remember the Polybius code? As you'll recall, it lays the letters in a special grid. The grid is the key here (see p58 for a Polybius refresher), and once you know this you can easily encode or decode a message, such as:

35, 42, 24, 32, 15

33, 45, 32, 12, 15, 42, 43

Of course, some agents are a little more devious than others. If you want to test your decoding skills to the maximum then try to create and decrypt double-coded messages! With these fiendish codes, once the first layer has been decoded it will resemble nonsense. However, this tangle of words (or numbers!) is another level of code. Tough, eh?

Our spy network has just intercepted this urgent double-coded message. Luckily the agent discovered the keys. The message was first encoded using a simple substitution cipher – numbering each letter. But then the second code was a Caesar's cipher that offset the letters by two places.

So, you start with this: **20, 7, 15, 7, 15, 4, 7, 20, 22, 17, 8, 7, 7, 6, 15, 1, 5, 3, 22**

Which leads to this:

TGOGODGTVQHGGFOAECV

Yikes! Using the second key, discovered by the agent, can you break the code?

There are much more complicated types of secret-key systems out there – such as a pre-shared key (PSK – you may see those letters if you have ever used a wi-fi connection) and a public-key, which is used to scramble messages over the internet. This all involves a lot of complicated maths, but at the heart of it all are the monsters of the number world: prime numbers.

PRIME NUMBERS

Maths doesn't come heavier than prime numbers.
But don't worry, you only need to know the basics!

31

7
5

47

37

59

13

43

23

19

41

61

31

Prime numbers are whole numbers that can
ONLY be divided by **ONE** and **THEMSELVES**.
That's it. The number 4 isn't a prime number
because it can be divided by 1, 2 and 4 – whereas
7 can only be divided by 1 and 7. Mathematicians
are constantly trying to discover the next prime
number. It's not an easy task. Here are a few:

**2, 3, 5, 7, 11, 13, 17, 19, 23, 29,
31, 37, 41, 43, 47, 53, 59, 61...**

That might sound easy, but the bigger the
numbers, the more difficult it is to discover. In
2015, the largest prime number is:

It might look weird, but it is a number that is so
large this book isn't big enough to print the full
number, which has 17,425,170 digits!

So what use are prime numbers? Because of
them you can buy stuff over the internet or send
top secret messages! This ingenious system
is called **RSA** (named after the three creators'
surnames), and it uses a complicated formula
and **TWO PRIME NUMBERS** as the key to
unlock the scrambled message.

61

37

47

23

11

59

53

59

43

53

13

19 23 23

31

11

59

47

As you might guess, this is very complex mathematics. It's so difficult that your top-secret cleared Maths teacher will just drool if you ask for an explanation. These numbers are so huge (and they use mathematical theorems with scary names like *Euler's totient function)* that computers are needed to work it all out.

SO HOW DOES IT WORK?

Back to the code! Take any two prime numbers and multiply them together – that's the key to encrypting your message. So, two prime numbers multiplied together – for example,

5231 X 7669 = ...

I'll wait while you get your calculator...

40,116,539.

Wow, that's a big number! Now to **DECRYPT** the message in order to read it, all you have to do is work out which two numbers I multiplied to get 40,116,539. Suddenly it's not very easy to work out, is it? Without knowing the **KEY**, it will take a very long time to crack the message.

That's the basic method for RSA encryption. Told you it was brain-boggling!

61

37 43 31 59

7

11

DIGITAL FOOTPRINTS

Every time you use the internet, you leave a trail of information. While you might think you're just posting a picture of your dinner on a social networking site, you have actually sent a LOT more information than you ever intended.

It is vital that all agents are cyber-aware, and know the consequences of their actions. By posting that simple picture here is what people can discover about you:

Sarah J Agent
7 March at 18:27 · Instagram

Check out my best ever dinner. Can't beat steak and chips! **#carnivore**

Like · Comment · Share

22 people like this

View 7 more comments

What the plate of food you had for dinner looks like. (Obviously!)

Your **NAME, AGE, HOME ADDRESS, EMAIL ADDRESS** – if you have unwisely put them onto the social media site when you registered.

Information on social media can be used for **PROFILING**. Potential snoops can find out who your friends and family are, if you're all connected.

As well as your dinner, they have **EVERY** other photograph you have posted – so they know what you look like. And if you delete it – **THE INFORMATION IS STILL THERE**!

Digital cameras insert **METADATA** into the photograph – which includes the type of camera used, the lighting levels in the room, when it was taken and (if your camera has GPS) where it was taken. You might be posting a picture of your dinner today but the metadata proves you ate it two weeks ago at a friend's house.

That's only some of the information you have just accidentally shared. Think what is on your computer that you haven't *intentionally* shared...

The **IP ADDRESS** of the computer you used – this is specific to your computer.

The **ROUTER ADDRESSES** of the computers your message passed through – this includes the local server and telephone exchange information, which can be used to **PINPOINT YOUR HOUSE**. It also has the **TIME** you sent the message – which proves *exactly* when and where you were at that moment.

On your computer you have:

CACHE HISTORY: This includes a record of internet sites you have visited. Caches are not just about the internet, your computer has cache histories of every program you have opened, and every time it has been switched on.

COOKIES: Not snacks, but files left on your computer by websites you have visited. They can contain information about what the website looks like and the passwords used to access it, which is why you don't have to retype your password when you return to the site.

Tracking cookies know where you have been. If you post a picture of your dinner on social media and then buy a book from an online shop, the shop's tracking cookies can read your social media cookie and see that you have posted the picture. The shop could now display a message asking if you would like to buy a cookbook!

DELETING DATA

You accidentally delete a file on the computer – nightmare! It might seem impossible to get it back, but it's not for a forensic computer expert. Using special software almost ANY information can be retrieved, even if you deleted it months ago.

When you delete a picture, the information **IS STILL THERE**. What is missing are the **FILE HEADERS** which the computer reads so that it knows *this is a picture of a cat*. Without the header, the computer ignores the picture. When you save something new, the computer seldom overwrites the old picture but just finds some free space elsewhere on your hard drive.

Specialist software can locate the data of your cat picture, put on new headers and reveal a picture you thought had been deleted. Internet servers operate this way too and they also regularly **BACKUP** their information, creating a history of what has been stored.

One way to destroy data once and for all is by running very strong magnets across a hard drive. This is not recommended for agents in training, however, as it will almost certainly destroy the hard drive as well!

REMEMBER: the internet works by **COPYING** information to pass along. Copies of your cat picture are still on your camera and computer. If you email it to a friend, it is now on your server, your friend's server (and their backups) and your friend's computer.

TOR

The Tor Project was created to help stop people being tracked online. The **ONION ROUTER** is a browser that allows you to be anonymous by hiding your IP address and other metadata. It achieves this by passing packets though multiple computers – like passing through the layers of an onion – each scrambling any attempt to locate you.

Tor is considered so safe that government agencies use it – but so do the bad guys. This has led to the unusual situation of the NSA and GCHQ having to hack the very system they are using if they want to spy on people.

METADATA

Metadata is basically data that describes other data so there's no problem there, right? Wrong! If you phone a friend on your mobile, your voice is turned into **DATA** and sent over the phone network. But there are all kinds of things attached to it, this is **METADATA**. It can include both phone numbers and types of phone, your location, your friend's location, if you are moving (remember **TRIANGULATION**?) and the time.

Supposing you called your doctor. Metadata is attached to that phone call – including that fact you have called a doctor. Now guesses can be made about you – are you ill? If not, is the doctor related to you? Why ring them in the first place? This is all good intel a spy can use to build a **PROFILE**.

PROFILING

During your spy missions you have been building files about your friends and family. You are building profiles about where they work and what they like. Your online habits help people build **PROFILES** about **YOU** and can reveal more than you intended.

Visiting funny cat photo webpages might indicate that you like cats and have a sense of humour. So if I want to catch your attention in the street, I should put up a large funny cat poster. While you stop and look at it, one of my agents can plant some incriminating evidence in your pocket!

CYBER ATTACK!

It is not just you who places lots of vital information on the internet – your parents, businesses and even governments do it as well. Plans, secrets and even vital financial information is now held online and the only way to get at it is by hacking. To protect yourself from hackers, you need to understand their tricks!

HACKERS

Hackers can write computer code that allows them to slip past online security and access the information being protected. A spy who is also a hacker is an invaluable asset for an intelligence agency. Hackers come in two basic types:

WHITE HATS: These hackers break into systems to test security. They don't take or damage information.

BLACK HATS: These are the guys who deliberately break into systems for sabotage and theft.

INTERNET SHADOWS

The term **DARKNET** was coined in the 1970s to describe any computer network that wasn't linked to **ARPANET.** This is the murky part of the internet where hackers trade information because it's harder to catch them.

Don't get this confused with the **DEEP WEB**, which are areas of the internet that are not recorded by search engines like Google. The mind-blowing truth is that the internet you use is the **SURFACE WEB** and to give you an idea of how small that is, you only see 0.03 per cent of what is out there. The rest lurks in the **DEEP WEB**.

It is here that criminals, hackers and spies create illegal websites that are incredibly difficult to trace.

FIREWALLS

While an actual wall of flame within your computer would be pretty cool, firewalls are much more useful than that! They protect computers from hackers trying to gain access. A firewall is computer program that sorts out packets of information that are trusted and secure. Occasionally you may get a message while online asking if you *trust* this website or cookie – that is your firewall speaking to you.

Internet

Firewall

Home network

THREATS

The internet is not just about storing information, intelligence agencies use it for sabotage too!

Every bank, power station, water dam and gas pipeline (even the ones connected to your house!) work on a computer network. By hacking these, power can be switched off – stopping your heating in the coldest winter and emptying your bank account!

Security cameras can be hacked, showing spies the inside of a building, bank vault or even nuclear power plant.

In 2014, a Russian website giving free access to webcams around the world was closed down. Although they hadn't been hacked, the owners hadn't set passwords, which meant anybody could access the webcams. They included baby-monitoring cameras and security cameras in shops and public spaces!

PASSWORDS

Make sure you password protect your computer, USB drives and even individual documents – but never write the password down!

A good password should have capital letters and numbers, jumbled up. Such as: pA55wOrd – but that's still not good enough. Try and use codes that aren't real words – so Kr66hA8oPPa would be MUCH better, although harder to remember. For even better security add some punctuation – how about Kr#66hA!8o?PPa?

But keep in mind that a highly secure password is only useful if you can actually remember it!

Name:

GARY MCKINNON

Going under the name of 'Solo', McKinnon is one of the world's most notorious hackers. From 2001, McKinnon spent 13 months hacking into 97 NASA and US Military computers – and he did it with ease. Was he looking for missile codes or secret agents' identities? No. He was searching for evidence that alien UFOs had visited Earth! Unfortunately for McKinnon he was caught and arrested by boring normal humans!

Name:

KEVIN POULSEN

Would you like a Porsche sports car? Kevin Poulsen did – and he came up with an ingenious (and very illegal) way to get one. Known by the hacker name 'Dark Dante', Poulsen hacked into a Los Angeles radio station's phone network – taking over all their phone lines – just so he could win the Porsche 944 they were giving away by guaranteeing he was the 102nd caller! The FBI later caught him.

Name:

THE UNKNOWN PRANKSTERS

In 2009, hackers gained access to road signs across America. Did they do it to cause mayhem and carnage? No. They posted a series of warnings, from 'RAPTORS AHEAD' through to 'ZOMBIES IN AREA! RUN!'

MALWARE

Imagine a computer program that was designed specifically to cause harm to your computer. Welcome to the world of malicious software, or malware.

There are many types of malware that you may come across, the most common being computer **VIRUSES**. Viruses are programs that hide within other programs and are designed to infect a computer, make copies of themselves and rapidly spread through a computer network to cause specific harm. You need to be careful!

While a majority of computer viruses are created by people trying to steal money, passwords or simply wanting to cause chaos, intelligence agencies also create their own.

In 2014, security companies raised the alarm on a virus called **REIGN**. It targeted computers in Saudi Arabia and Russia and appeared to gather data for mass surveillance rather than cause any harm. It is thought that Reign had been spying for eight years before it was finally identified. This type of malware is referred to as **SPYWARE**.

ZOMBIES

These zombies are not the living dead, but computers under the control of hackers using malware. You may not even be aware that your computer is a zombie as it will operate normally. However, the hacker can hijack it to send emails or data – marked with your IP address – around the world.

ANONYMOUS

Since 2003 a group of hacker activists **(HACKTIVISTS)** loosely joined together to form the group **ANONYMOUS**. These elite hackers gather and distribute information – often secret or personal – and publicly release it, believing that it is for the greater good.

DOS WARFARE

DENIAL OF SERVICE ATTACKS are temporary attacks on a computer system. There are multiple ways of creating a DoS attack, but one of the most common is for hackers to use thousands of zombie computers to send millions of messages to a server. The server can't handle the sudden demand and either crashes or slows down so much that it's useless! This could disable a building's security computers, allowing a spy to quickly enter without triggering alarms.

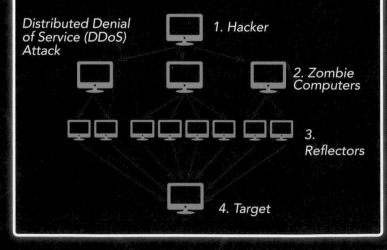

Distributed Denial of Service (DDoS) Attack

1. Hacker

2. Zombie Computers

3. Reflectors

4. Target

TROJANS

Trojan computer viruses take their name from a Greek legend. During the battle of Troy, the Greek army pretended to surrender and left a huge wooden horse at the Trojans' gates. The Trojans, obviously not being very bright, thought it was a gift and brought it into the city. What they didn't realise was that Greek soldiers were hiding inside. As night fell, the Greeks sneaked out of the horse and opened the gates so the rest of their army could invade.

This is exactly how a computer Trojan works, without the Greeks, Trojans or giant horses, of course!

Trojans can be planted on a computer via an unsuspecting user opening a file attached to an email. The file is really a Trojan program that is activated and hides on the computer until it is needed. Some computer security systems are so strong that spies often have to plant the Trojan themselves, usually carrying it on a USB drive.

When a hacker wants to access your Trojan-infected computer, they give the hacker-equivalent of a secret knock. The Trojan bypasses your virus checker and firewall and simply opens up without you ever being aware of it. Now the hacker-spy can read every document on your computer and even see exactly what is on the screen.

File Download - Security Warning ☒

Do you want to run or save this file?

Name: World_AV_Setup_RW.exe
Type: Application, 8.45MB
From: Lonelyplanet.com

[Run]   [Save]   [Cancel]

⚠ While files from the internet can be useful, this file type can potentially harm your computer. If you do not trust the source, do not run or save this software.

UP CLOSE AND PERSONAL

Near Field Communication (NFC) is a very convenient technology that allows people to pay for things by passing a card over a reader.

You may have one already – from borrowing a library book, buying lunch in the school canteen, or travelling on buses and trains. A small chip in the card communicates with a sensor and the payment is made. Simple, convenient and completely traceable by a spy!

Remember: all data is stored somewhere. So when you swipe a card to board an underground train, and again when you exit, a record has been made of exactly what time you entered and left as well as the locations. Unlike wi-fi signals, NFC signals have a small range – just a centimetre or so – which makes them more difficult to detect. Remember the wi-fi rock MI5 left in Russia? It would have been less detectable using NFC connection, which an agent would just have to brush past to transfer the intelligence.

BIG BROTHER

Somebody is watching you! In some countries it is difficult to walk out of the door without being watched! Mass surveillance is everywhere.

The term Big Brother is used to indicate that the government or other official bodies are watching your every move. It comes from the book *1984* by George Orwell, which describes a country in which the citizens are under constant surveillance!

The UK is one of the most watched countries in the world with 5.9 million cameras – that's one camera for every 11 people who live there!

Cameras come in all shapes and sizes. Some have microphones to record conversations, others have nightvision capabilities. They are controlled from a local command centre, whose staff are watching for suspicious activity and can initiate a rapid police response.

I KNOW THAT FACE...

Another huge step in surveillance is **FACIAL RECOGNITION SOFTWARE**. Computers can scan video footage of crowds and, using **BIOMETRICS**, can pick out your face in a busy crowd.

Government agencies can tap into local surveillance cameras and study the video to pick out a specific target.

SURVEILLANCE IN ACTION!

Throughout your training you have seen how the big international spy agencies have huge technological resources to spy on other countries. Let's take a look at a few of the cyber tools they use.

PRISM

The USA has a massive electronic surveillance program called Prism, run by the NSA, that sucks-up internet communications, such as emails and metadata, all of which can be analyzed later by agents.

Prism's existence was Top Secret until 2013 when Edward Snowden (see page 21) leaked it.

XKEYSCORE

There is so much information passing through Prism that people can never sort through it all. Instead, a computer system called **XKS** (**XKEYSCORE**) scans it all for anything it considers suspicious.

XKeyscore can read anyone's email and track people – including you – building a **DIGITAL FINGERPRINT**. With this fingerprint you can be found anywhere on the internet, instantly.

Russia has its own system called **SORM** (System for Operative Investigative Activities), while almost every other country has their own similar Top Secret mass surveillance programs they don't want you to know about!

DISHFIRE

While Prism collects internet data, another NSA program called **DISHFIRE** was created to collect your phone's **TEXT MESSAGES**. Hundreds of millions of them. They are then analyzed for secret information by a system known as **PREFER**.

TEMPORA

Britain's GCHQ has Tempora. This high-tech system intercepts information passing through the internet's fibre-optic cables that run under the ocean.

Tempora stores phone conversations (remember, once you speak into a phone your voice is converted into data), emails, and social media messages. In fact, it stores everything!

SPYING ON YOUR FRIENDS

Remember your debrief about **FIVE EYES** back when you were a recruit? Allied countries working together makes a formidable collection of intelligence, but that still doesn't stop allied countries spying on each other.

In 2014, it was revealed that the USA had been intercepting German Chancellor Angela Merkel's mobile phone conversations and messages. This strained relationships between the two countries and made the rest of the world wonder who is spying on who.

PROTECT YOURSELF

Your training is almost complete. You have learned many skills that can be used at home, in the field and online. All of these skills can be combined together for you to become a full Secret Agent.

For example, the only real way of avoiding Big Brother surveillance cameras is to wear a disguise like the one in Chapter 5 – facial recognition software is very difficult to beat!

Remember all your tradecraft – try to take different routes to your destination, rather than repeat the same path.

While on an operation, always pay for your tickets using cash rather than NFC or credit cards. Cash is still pretty untraceable.

Mobile phones

Out in the field, agents use **BURNER** phones. These are regular pay-as-you go phones that have not been registered to any user. An agent will know exactly who has been given the number to their burner phone, so if any unexpected calls are received then there is something wrong!

The smart thing to do when engaging in covert operations is to turn your phone off, right? Wrong. Malware can fake switching a phone off and, even if it really was off, your phone could still be monitored.

SECURE WEBSITES

If you look in the address bar of an internet browser you will see the letters HTTP. This is a regular unsecure website. If you are planning to shop online or enter personal information you want to ensure the website is secure. This is easy enough, just check that the URL now reads: **HTTPS**. The extra 's' means the connection between your computer and the website is **SECURE** and will probably have a padlock icon to indicate that.

Mission briefing

It's important that you and your new spy ring are protected every time you go online. Follow these steps to avoid cyber surveillance:

 Create **DIFFICULT PASSWORDS** to secure your computer, email, social media, etc. Also ensure that the password for your wi-fi connection is strong. But make sure you remember them!

 NEVER give out your passwords to anybody – **EVER**.

 Install a **VIRUS CHECKER** and keep it up to date. In addition, use programs that detect malware, such as **SPYBOT**.

 Make sure your computer's **FIREWALL** is turned on.

 NEVER open attachments from people you don't know - it could be malware!

 NEVER post personal details online. It's not essential to share your birthday and definitely don't give phone numbers or your home address to any website!

 Constantly **DELETE** your web history and cookies.

COVER your webcam up when not in use.

If in doubt **DISCONNECT** from the internet immediately.

And remember – if you're using a computer that is not your own, always log-out of email accounts, social media, etc and delete the computer's history and cookies. This will stop the next person accessing your stuff!

TRACK THE AGENT!

Your agency has been tracking a Super Spy, but has lost him in this village. Using the GEOINT below, use your skills to answer the questions and get back on his trail. It will take all your observation and tracking skills to accomplish the mission! Answers are on page157 if you get stuck.

1) How did the agent arrive in the village?

5) We think the agent received further orders while in town, but we can't work out how. Can you analyze the image and let us know how?

4) We managed to eventually retrieve the intel the spy hid in his dead drop. It is his code name, but can you decipher it?

⌐⊓⊓·> ⊏⊐⊔·⊓

3) Can you identify the dead drop the spy used?
2) What colour coat were they wearing?

THE SPY CHALLENGE!

Before you can complete your training, you have a final Spy Challenge to complete. You can find the answers on page 157. Remember, no cheating – we will be watching!

1   What did the Soviet Union's KGB spy agency change to?

2   What was the name of German Agent known as the Sardine Spy?
    a) Hans Gruber
    b) Edward Snowden
    c) Ludovico Zender

3   Decode the name of this location:
    UAFPGA, CWUVTCNKC

4   What nickname do agents give the CIA?

5   Arrange the security ranks into the correct order of secrecy:

    Secret, Official, Restricted

6   Write TOP SECRET in Morse code.

7   What does DARPA stand for?

8   What is a UAV more commonly known as?

9   What nationality was Agent Rose?

10 What does SIGINT stand for?

You need 7 out of 10 to pass – if you fail the test, then you must go back and re-read the relevant chapters again!

MISSION COMPLETE!

CONGRATULATIONS, YOUR TRAINING IS OVER.

YOU ARE NO LONGER A
FIELD AGENT
YOU ARE NOW A FULLY FLEDGED

SECRET AGENT!

BUT THIS IS NOT THE END – IT'S ONLY THE BEGINNING OF YOUR SPY CAREER. YOUR FINAL MISSION IS TO KEEP YOUR AGENCY ACTIVE – ALWAYS BE ON THE LOOKOUT FOR SUSPICIOUS ACTIVITY!

A GOOD AGENT LOOKS FOR THE CHANCE TO IMPROVE THEIR SKILLS. ALWAYS BE PREPARED FOR AN OPPORTUNITY TO USE THESE VITAL TALENTS IN YOUR EVERYDAY LIFE AND MAYBE, ONE DAY, YOU WILL BE THE SECRET AGENT WHO SAVES YOUR COUNTRY! OF COURSE, NOBODY WILL EVER KNOW... BUT YOU WILL.

GOOD LUCK – AND GOOD SPYING!

GLOSSARY

Biometrics – The analysis of human characteristics, such as facial features and fingerprints.

Bug – An electronic device allowing agents to listen in on others' conversations.

Cipher – A type of code where one letter or number is substituted for another.

Cold War – A war fought between the Soviet Union and its allies and America and its allies, in which no fighting took place.

Covert – Actions or missions that are kept secret.

Credentials – Proof of your identity.

Cryptanalysis – Cracking coded messages without a key.

Decoy – A method of distracting a pursuer or enemy agent.

Defector – A spy who switches sides while still in service.

Drone – An unmanned aircraft that can be piloted from many miles away.

Enigma – The name given to the fiendishly difficult code machine used in World War II.

Espionage – The professional term for the act of spying.

Forensics – Tests used to investigate and detect crimes.

Malware – Programs developed specifically to do harm to computers.

Mark – A target or suspect assigned to an agent.

Off the grid – The state of being unconnected to services such as electricity, and being untraceable by technology.

Photon – A single particle of light used in quantum encryption.

Satellite – An object sent into orbit to collect or relay information

Sleeper – An agent who is undercover for a long time, but is only activated to start spying when necessary.

Soviet Union – A group of countries, including Russia, united under one communist state, which was dissolved in 1991.

Spy ring – A group of spies working together.

Spyware – A type of malware used by intelligence agencies to gather information from computers.

Stealth – Moving very cautiously or quietly so as not to be seen.

Steganography – The art of hiding something in plain sight.

Tail – Someone following you.

Virus – A piece of code that can copy itself many times over to do harm to a computer and destroy data.

65% 81% 32% 96% 53%

ANSWERS for p154:
1) The FSB
2) c) Ludovico Zender
3) SYDNEY, AUSTRALIA
4) The Farm
5) Official, Restricted, Secret
6) - --- .-.   ... .. -.-.- -
7) Defense Advanced Research Projects Agency
8) A drone
9) French
10) Signal Intelligence

ANSWERS for p152:
1) By bicycle.
2) Yellow
3) Under the bench
4) Agent Fang
5) He was receiving orders through a Numbers radio station

INDEX

MIX
Paper from responsible sources
FSC™ C021741

Paper in this book is certified against the Forest Stewardship Council™ standards. FSC™ promotes environmentally responsible, socially beneficial and economically viable management of the world's forests.